T0106849

# After
## *Ever*
## After

# After *Ever* After

Finding and Keeping the Love of a Lifetime

## Tom Boomershine *with* Winter

ARCHWAY
PUBLISHING

Cover art by Abraham Corona

Archway Publishing books may be ordered through booksellers or by contacting:

Archway Publishing
1663 Liberty Drive
Bloomington, IN 47403
www.archwaypublishing.com
1 (888) 242-5904

ISBN: 978-1-4808-4836-8 (sc)
ISBN: 978-1-4808-4837-5 (hc)
ISBN: 978-1-4808-4838-2 (e)

Library of Congress Control Number: 2017911036

Print information available on the last page.

Archway Publishing rev. date: 12/1/2017

# Contents

# Introduction

How do you find and keep the love of a lifetime? Do you belong to a dating website? Are you on a diet or exercising like a fiend to have that perfect body in order to attract a partner? Or both? Think about the time, money, and emotional energy you spend trying to find the man or woman you want to spend your life with. Once you've found him or her, how do you keep that love alive? According to the American Psychological Association, 40-50 percent of marriages end in divorce. Trust me. You don't want to get a divorce. Whoever wrote the adage, "It's better to love and have lost than to never have loved" did not get a divorce. It's better to be single and searching than married and miserable. I had one of the easiest, gentlest, most equitable divorces I have ever heard of, and it sucked so bad that it boggles the mind!

♪ Ed Sheeran, "Thinking Out Loud"

## My Greatest Wish

I have been a United Methodist pastor for almost twenty years and have counseled and married more than one hundred couples. This is the book I wish they all had before they started dating. In it you will be shown: the secret to finding a great partner, how to avoid overcommitting so that you save yourself for the person you can love forever—the two bedrock foundations that will make or break your marriage—and how to protect your relationship so you can keep it forever.

My greatest wish for every couple I marry, and the best blessing I can give them is, "I hope you have a relationship like my wife and mine." Winter and I have been married for fourteen years. Over and over again, people come to us (well, mostly to Winter) and ask, "You both seem really happy. How do you do it?" They are right. We are happy, very happy as a couple and as individuals. This book shows how we found and kept each other. This book is how we do it.

I promise you, if you follow the principles outlined in this book, you will be happier, more comfortable in your own skin, more attractive to potential partners, and able to find and keep the love of a lifetime.

Before you spend a minute longer exercising, dieting, or trolling

> *This book will prepare you to get lucky—not just for a night but forever.*

dating websites, read this book! Don't wait anymore. He or she is out there somewhere. The Roman philosopher Seneca said, "Luck is what happens when preparation meets opportunity." This book will prepare you to get lucky—not just for a night but forever.

**What the Special Notations Are About**

I had music running through my head as I wrote many parts of this book. If you like to listen to music while reading, you can enter the titles on YouTube or your favorite online music station like Spotify and listen to what I was hearing as I was writing. They provide additional insight into my thoughts and feelings., If you don't like listening to music while reading or find it too distracting, please feel free to ignore the music references and read in blissful silence.

# *Chapter 1*

## Your Objective

Marriage to the right person is heaven. Marriage to the wrong person is hell. I've been in both. I am so happy to be in heaven now and to have lived there for 16 years. I will show you, step by step, how to find and keep the love you have been looking for. A partner who loves you for you, "All your curves and all your edges, all your perfect imperfections," as John Legend writes.

Let's face it: none of us is perfect. I've got warts. When I get up from writing this and take a shower, I'm going to be looking at those warts. Or better yet, if I hop in bed before the shower and get naked with my beautiful wife, she's going to be looking at those warts. She loves me, warts and all. Because she loves me for all my strengths and weaknesses, I get to be more me, more Tom Boomershine, than I am when it's just me, myself, and I. This is the promise of the love of a lifetime—getting to be more you because of the support of a true partner in life.

♪ John Legend, "All of Me"

♪ De La Soul, "Me, Myself and I"

1

That's what you want, a real, true-to-life, full-blown partner; someone you can be naked with physically, emotionally, and spiritually and feel supported, appreciated, and accountable to.

## Free to Be Me

You've got warts; we all have warts. Whether literally or metaphorically, we all have strengths and weaknesses—physically, emotionally, and personally. Nobody is a great engineer with amazing vision who paints better than Picasso and is the glue holding together all the relationships of their organization while taking care of all the little details.

> *You don't want to be loved for an ideal version of you that you have to work tirelessly to maintain, denying parts of you for the sake of someone else's expectations.*

None of us is wired like that. You don't want to be loved for an ideal version of you that you have to work tirelessly to maintain, denying parts of you for the sake of someone else's expectations. You want to love and be loved for who you are. You want to be the best you that you can be, and you want to love someone else in the same way—for who they are. This is the essence of the love of a lifetime. This is your objective.

## Love

What is love, anyway? Is love that heart-palpitating feeling when you see the object of your desire across a crowded room? Is love like the advisor said to the king in *Cinderella*:

"He sees her across a crowded room. There she stands. The girl of his dreams. Who she is and whence she came he knows not nor does he care, but his heart tells him here is the maid predestined to be his bride." Is that true love? What is this love most of us seek, desire, sweat, and bleed to attain, yet often fail to keep?

If we buy into the prevailing culture around us, we believe love is a feeling, something that we can fall into and out of. Love is attraction and romance and desire and passion. This is fun while it lasts, but the truth and fact of the matter is, our feelings can be and often are fleeting and fickle. It's much like what I feel like eating. Today, I'm in the mood for Italian; tomorrow, Mexican; Wednesday, sushi; and Friday, "Ohhh! Vegetarian sounds good." Variety is the spice of life, right? This is why many of us hop from one relationship to the next, doing all kinds of emotional damage to others and ourselves.

*Howard Jones, "What Is Love Anyway"*

## Covenant and Committed Love

What if there was a way to keep the fire burning? What if there was something more, something deeper, filled with a fire that burns hot some days and simmers on others? What if you could have a partner in life? Someone who, regardless of what is going on, irrespective of how you or they are feeling, through internal and external highs and lows, would stick with you and care for you, no matter what is going on? Someone who you know and who knows you inside, outside, and upside down and cares for you in spite of— and often because of—your quirks and flaws and failures? Someone who won't abandon you when the next bit of tasty "food" is offered up to you on an appealing platter? And you would return that same kind of care.

Now we're starting to get into an entirely different zone. This is love based on a promise, a commitment; love that doesn't depend on how anybody is feeling, but instead depends on an action; love that is a choice. Love as behavior; covenant or promised, love. This is what we commit to when we get married, at least in the Judeo-Christian faiths. When we say, "In the name of God, I take you, to have and to hold, for richer or for poorer, for better or for worse, in sickness and in health, to love and to cherish until we are parted by death," we are committing to an action. Regardless of how we are feeling on a moment-by-moment basis, we promise we will care for our lover, come what may, period. This love is unique, so special, so sacred that the Roman Catholic Church considers it a sacrament, which means they believe the very love of God for each and every one of us is revealed through the promise we make to each other when we get married. God will never leave us; God will always care for us. God is always faithful. Covenant love—this is what we commit to when we get married.

### Love: An Action, Not a Feeling

Stephen Covey is one of my favorite self-help authors. For about five years, I read or listened to *The Seven Habits of Highly Effective People* at least once every year. In it, he tells the story of a man who asked him what he could do about his marriage. He approached Covey during one of his seminars, saying that while he liked what Covey was saying, he wasn't sure how it would apply to his situation. He stated that he and his wife no longer loved each other, and they were worried about their kids. What should they do? Covey told him, "Love her." Thinking Covey didn't understand, he clarified that the feeling of love just wasn't there anymore. Covey said, "My friend, love is a verb. Love—the feeling—is a fruit of love, the verb. So love her. Serve her. Sacrifice. Listen to her. Empathize. Appreciate. Affirm her. Are you willing to do that?"

If love is an action, then love is a choice that we choose and control. On many levels, we can't control our emotions. If love is only a feeling, then it's out of our hands, and keeping the love of a lifetime often becomes extremely difficult, if not impossible. But the love of a lifetime is a choice, an action, a behavior that we can choose *regardless* of how we feel. As Covey outlines, the more we behave in loving ways to our chosen partner, the more we feel loving. In an exercise later in this book, we will explore ways to choose love and act loving on a moment-by-moment basis and the effect that this has on "keeping the love of a lifetime."

> *Love is a verb. Love—the feeling—is a fruit of love, the verb.*
> —Stephen Covey

If your objective is to find and keep the love of a lifetime, there are some things you need to do. Before you go on a date, before you start trolling profiles on "farmerswholove-businesspeople.com," before you allow your mom or best friend to set you up, you need to work on you. It all begins with you.

Winter's Thoughts: Thomas claims variety is the spice of life, and he's absolutely correct. However, variety does not need to come in the form of different partners. If you give your partner the gift of loving them completely for who they are and allowing them to grow into that, it will take a life-

> *Variety and spice comes from growing, becoming more fully who you are, and encouraging your partner to do the same. —Winter*

time to truly know each other. Variety and spice comes from growing, becoming more fully who you are, and encouraging your partner to do the same. As you both grow and change, you get to learn new things about each other every day of your lives together. You get the comfort, depth, and coziness of a long-term partner. You also get the excitement of learning new things because you haven't locked your partner into your ideal of who they should be. It is the best way to deepen who you are, so there's always more to experience.

# Chapter 2

## Love Yourself

You are worthy of love and inimitably loveable. You deserve the love of a lifetime and nothing less. You are beautiful and valuable. Nobody in the world is just like you. Nobody can do the things you were made to do by God. Only you can offer the gift of *you* to life. If you have trouble believing the reality of the previous statements, if you don't love yourself, nobody else can truly love you. They cannot love you because you cannot receive love. You cannot receive somebody else's love because you don't believe them. When they say, "I love you," somewhere in your mind, you say, "No, you don't."

It's time for a reality check. It is time to get naked—literally, emotionally, and spiritually.

## Exercise 1: Getting Naked

Lock the doors. Take off all your clothes. Stand in front of a full-length mirror and take stock. Look at yourself. Can you see how beautiful you are, all that is perfect and imperfect? This is the real-deal beauty!

Now get out a *Cosmopolitan* magazine or *GQ* or the like. Look at the picture of one of those models and say, "You are stinkin' thinkin'!" Because it is. That photo has been Photoshopped within an inch of its life. Nobody looks like the models in the magazines, including the models themselves. One of the most well-known super-models of all time, Cindy Crawford said in a 1993 *People* magazine article, "Even I don't wake up looking like Cindy Crawford."

Do a Google search on "the reality of celebrity photoshop before and after." The industry is arguing that "Everybody knows that the pictures are Photoshopped, so it shouldn't be a big deal." It *is* a big deal. What gets your attention gets you. If you are filling your mind with images of beauty that are literally unattainable, it has an effect, and the effect is all around us.

### Profit Motive for Low Self-Esteem

Kendra Hodgson, in the study guide to *Killing Us Softly 4* says it best:

> Ads create an environment. Just as it's dif-
> ficult to be healthy in a toxic physical en-
> vironment, if we're breathing poisoned air
> or drinking polluted water, it's difficult to
> be healthy in a "toxic cultural environment"

♪ Joe Cocker, "You Can Leave Your Hat On"

that surrounds us with unhealthy images and constantly sacrifices our health and well-being for the sake of profit. All the polls show that the self-esteem of women and girls is steadily decreasing over time. This is starting to become the case for boys, too. Which is exactly what corporations are gunning for and hope. The more dissatisfied we all become with ourselves, the more money there is to be made.

Our consumer economy of "profit at any cost" makes tons of money by lowering our self-esteem. My favorite illustration of this is the Old Spice "<u>look at your man</u>" commercials from a couple of years ago. Put down this book and watch the ad or ads on YouTube now.

You laughed. I laughed. We all laughed. Old Spice names, claims, and owns it in a very entertaining way. What Old Spice is owning is what we all need to name and claim. We are bombarded by messages every day that intentionally, systematically, and systemically lower our self-esteem because the less happy we are with ourselves, our family, our kids, and our partners, the more money there is to be made. This, my dear reader, is indeed "stinkin' thinkin'."

We cannot avoid advertising. None of us can. It's everywhere. If you watch the YouTube videos I suggest, you will be forced to watch at least a portion of an ad first. If you go to the supermarket, you are bombarded with ads in the forms of the covers of magazines. These magazines demand that you be vicariously dissatisfied with yourself through the collective shaming we are encouraged to participate in. The covers of countless magazines tout how one celebrity or another is too skinny, too fat, too hot, or too not. Yet each and every image is an out-and-out lie, Photoshopped to prove whatever headline it is touting—all serving the purpose of getting us to buy more crap we don't need!

There are countless products we don't need that all this advertising promotes by ensuring our perpetual and ever-increasing low self-esteems. Just think about all the beauty, fitness, and medical products to "fix" something in or on our bodies that really doesn't need fixing. Why are our kids killing themselves with greater frequency? Well, at least in part, it's because they have deeply bought what is being sold: "You are not enough."

### You Are More than Enough

Meghan Trainor's song, "All about That Bass" is a song about personal empowerment. In the song, she's clearly taking great pride in her body and the way it's made. "I'm all about that bass, no treble." Get some, Meghan Trainor! But maybe *you* aren't all about that bass. Maybe you're all about that treble, or that face or hair or whatever. The point is to love you for who you are and how you are made.

Here's how insidious our culture is. Winter and I were watching the 2014 year in review with Kathy Lee Gifford on New Year's Eve. Kathy and the other women were saying that 2014 was "All about That Bass" showing pictures of Kim Kardashian and Nicki Minaj, all to Meghan Trainor's song. Then Kathy said something like,

"Isn't it ironic that 2014 is all about the bass. I have spent my whole lifetime exercising trying to get rid of my bass."

Do you see how crazy this all is? If we try to mold our bodies into the prevailing view of popular culture at the moment, we will spend endless dollars dieting, bulking up, or slimming down. Boob jobs to increase our busts. Boob jobs to decrease our busts. Booty jobs to bulk up our booties, then booty jobs to decrease our booties, and, and, and. Do you see how many different people are making money off of our dissatisfaction with our bodies and how it never ends?

♪ Public Enemy, "Fight the Power"

So, what do we do? This stinkin' thinkin' gets inside us, and when we look in the mirror, often we don't see the beautiful person who is right in front of us. We see and hear all the critiques we are bombarded with on a moment-by-moment basis: "I'm too fat. I'm too skinny. My butt is too big. My butt is too small. My breasts are too small. My breasts are too big. I'm too short. I'm too tall." The list goes on and on and on endlessly.

*If we try to mold our bodies into the prevailing view of popular culture at the moment, we will spend endless dollars dieting, bulking up, or slimming down.*

Why? Because someone has a product you can buy that will fix that!

You are enough. You are more than enough. You are fantastic and beautiful. It's no wonder you can't see it. You are told in thousands of ways each and every day by multiple sources that you are inadequate.

## The Fix

We need an outside authority, somebody or something bigger than us that we believe to be the voice of real truth. We
need the ultimate reality check, something that peels back
all the stuff on the surface and helps us peer underneath
what we see around us on a daily basis, so we can see what
is really going on beneath the surface of our culture. We
need God.

There are many gods to choose from. There are the
gods of pop culture, of money, of sex and power, but
they're all trying to
sell us something,         *If it ain't healthy,*
to use us for their          *it ain't of God.*
purpose. There are
many different un-
derstandings of God in the great faith traditions. The
God I believe in as a United Methodist pastor is a God of
perfect love who is all about, and only about, what makes
life healthy, whole, and well. "If it ain't healthy, it ain't
of God."

This God loves us unconditionally. We cannot do anything to make God not love us, because we are God's children, shaped and formed by God's loving hands in our
mother's wombs; the breath of life was "breathed" into us by
God's own breath. In the eyes of God, we are perfect, even
in our imperfections.

## Imperfection Is What Makes You Uniquely Beautiful

In fact, in many ways it is our imperfections that make us
perfect. This is what it is to be human—perfectly imperfect.
Think about it: What gives somebody else character? What

makes you an individual? What separates you and makes you distinctly you? It's not the ways that you are like other people—it's the ways that you are different. The model of perfection presented to us by our culture is the same. It would make us all look the same; the same surgically enhanced boobs, the same impossibly small waist, the same flawless skin, the same six-pack abs. That's what Photoshop does—it makes people who look different and unique look more like some idealized version of humanity that really is not human.

It is our differences, which are more often than not labeled "flaws" or "imperfections," that make us unique individuals. Often these "flaws" and "imperfections" are our greatest strengths. Where would Lea Michele, who played Rachel Berry on *Glee*, be if she had gotten the nose job she was told she had to have in order to be a successful actress?

Let's move off the physical. I am loud, particularly my laugh. My friends and family find me in darkened theaters and crowded rooms by echolocation. One time I was meeting a buddy at a movie. He ended up running late and was looking for me in a crowded, darkened movie theater. What to do? He simply waited for some funny part of the movie and, "Ah! There's Tom!" My wife says, "Some people giggle, titter, or guffaw. You cachinnate," (which means "to laugh immoderately").

Some people describe my laughter as a flaw. I can't tell you the number of people who have tried to shush me or given me dirty looks at some theatrical performance. I suppose if I were in the special operations of some military service behind enemy lines, this would be a major liability.

But I have to say, if my tombstone reads, "He was known by his laughter," I can live with that.

## Weaknesses = Strength/Strength = Weakness

Strength or weakness, it's all contextual. Every week, I speak in front of large groups of people. Is it a strength to be vocally loud? You bet! Is it a liability when one of my family members is sleeping in and I'm talking with somebody in the kitchen? It is indeed.

This is not to say that there aren't areas where we all can and should improve. One of the professors at my college, Hugh Barbour, was a brilliant professor of religion. He and William Frost wrote one of the definitive histories of American Quakerism. Hugh was a legend at Earlham College, not only for his teaching and intellect but as the quintessential absent-minded professor. He lectured in a suit and tie, keeping a handkerchief in the inside pocket of his suit jacket. Apparently, he had bad allergies all the time, because he was always reaching inside his jacket to get the handkerchief to blow his nose. Invariably, after about the third or fourth time of going for the handkerchief, he'd miss, grab his tie, blow his nose and stuff the end of his tie in the pocket of his jacket.

Apparently, one day Hugh's wife called the registrar, asking where his paychecks were. When the registrar asked what she meant, she said Hugh hadn't been paid for three months! Clearly, Earlham College had not managed to figure out how to avoid paying one of its tenured professors for three months, so the registrar and his wife started looking through his office. Drawer after drawer, file after file refused to yield the sought-after checks until they found on his desk a scholarly tome with a number of bookmarks sticking out of the end. There were the paychecks!

When life becomes unmanageable because of a weakness or a flaw, that's when you might think about changing it. For Hugh, not depositing his paychecks could have led to financial and relational dis-ease with himself and his loved ones. He may have wanted to figure out some kind of system to make sure his paychecks are put in the bank. Similarly, if you are eating too much sugar and fat or too much in general, you might want to figure out a way to eat a healthy diet.

The objective is always to move toward greater health. So, if we identify that our regular eating habits are unhealthy, change *the habits* to something that is healthier. Changing habits is tough, really tough. That's why the vast majority of us never lose weight and keep it off. This takes us back to God, an outside authority who has our best interests, our health and wellness, and what makes us the beautiful people we are, always at heart.

## Exercise 2: You Are So Beautiful

Go back in front of that mirror, naked again. Look again at yourself through God's eyes, and listen to God sing to you through Joe Cocker. You are beautiful. Worthy of the love of a lifetime and nothing less. Live it. Walk it. Own it. Never settle.

> *You are beautiful. Worthy of the love of a lifetime and nothing less. Live it. Walk it. Own it. Never settle.*

♪ Joe Cocker, "You Are So Beautiful"

## Act As If

You may still be struggling to see yourself as beautiful. When you look at the cover of *Cosmopolitan* or *GQ* or other magazines, you may think, *"If only I looked like that,"* or *"if only this part of me was bigger or smaller"* or something else that is a bad comparison. If any of the above is the case, it is time to act as if ...

We have wonderful brains that believe whatever we tell them. How we talk to ourselves and about other people makes a huge difference in what we believe and eventually see. If we constantly tell ourselves, "I'm ugly," or if we focus on different areas of our body or personality that we don't like, that is what we will see, and that is what we will believe. Don't engage in negative self-talk. As Tony Horton of P90X fame says, "Never say 'I can't.' Say, 'I currently struggle with.'" If we tell ourselves, "I'm beautiful" over and over again, slowly, over time, we will see it. Start with one thing you like about yourself. Affirm it repeatedly, and build from there until you love all of you.

## Exercise 3: Act As If

Every morning, when you wake up and look in the mirror, look yourself in the eyes and say out loud, "Good morning, beautiful." Whenever you look in the mirror during the day, say, "Hello, beautiful." Whenever you look at one of the fashion or gossip magazines or a billboard and there's that self-critical voice that says, "I wish ..." or "If only ..." or "This part of me is ugly ..." immediately say, "That's stinkin' thinkin'. I'm beautiful."

**Winter's view:** About twenty years ago, I realized the negative impact our society's advertising was having on the self-esteem of young women. I decided to do everything I could to counter the attack. I began offering compliments, *sincere compliments only*, whenever I could: "I like the way you think," or "It is endearing to hear the way you talk about your kids," or "You have a great smile," or "You are lovely," or "That color looks fantastic on you," and so on.

I expected this to be difficult for me, since I struggled with self-esteem issues myself. I worried that I would feel even more inadequate when I began affirming other women's attributes. Oddly, I found the opposite result. I began to feel better about myself. I look at old photos of myself. I was a stunningly pretty young woman, but I felt inadequate and unattractive. I was too busty, too short, too ethnic-looking, and my hips were too wide. And that hair! I affectionately refer to it as "the Beast." Crikey, on humid days I worried it would put someone's eye out! Now I'm older and rounder; gravity has worked its magic. I have wrinkles and graying hair. I feel beautiful. Most days, I feel positively gorgeous.

As I was able to recognize and affirm other women's beauty and strengths, I was also able to embrace my own. You can use this in all of your relationships. Affirm and appreciate your loved ones, flaws and all. It allows them to be fully who they are. It allows you to be fully who you are as well.

# Chapter 3

## Your Stuff

There's a theory in psychology, popularized by Dr. Harville Hendrix in his book, *Getting the Love You Want.* Hendrix suggests that we marry our partners not so much for their positive characteristics but for their negative ones. Particularly, we recognize in our partner something that is unresolved from our childhood, with one or both of our parents that we need to resolve.

### My Stuff

Let me give you a picture of how I have seen this in my own life. In every significant long-term relationship I have had, my partner has experienced some kind of abuse in her past. When I look at my family history, my father tells me my great-grandfather was apparently insane. He abused laxatives, was an alcoholic, and regularly beat my grandfather with a leather strap. The final straw for my grandfather was an incident when the cows got left out in the field. My great-grandfather beat my grandfather so severely, he left home at the age of fourteen and never went back.

As far as I know, my grandfather was never physically abusive to my father or my aunt, but he was a wicked teaser. Most of the time, it was all fun and games, but every once in a while, there was a zinger that was not funny—not a joke. It hurt.

My father was neither physically abusive, nor did he tease in mean ways. But my dad, my younger brother, and I had this weird competition over food. For example, Mom made whatever birthday cake we wanted for our birthdays. All three of us loved the same kind of cake—chocolate with Grandma's caramel icing. Mmm, mmm, mmmm! On our birthdays, we would share the cake, but whatever was left over was supposed to be a gift to the birthday boy, to be eaten—shared or not shared—according to his wishes and desires. Each of us loved his cake. Each of us often froze a quarter or even half the cake so that we could eat it at our leisure, and each of us sneaked into the freezer and stole portions of the other one's cake! This is how we related to food in my family of origin. To this day, my brother refuses to share *his* French fries with his wife and kids because of the trauma from this part of our family craziness.

## The Family Jewels

I am still trying to work out the craziness in me stemming from the physical abuse of my great-grandfather on my grandfather. Thankfully, each generation of my forefathers has done a lot better than the previous generation, so the family is getting healthier over time—but it's still there. I think this is why we see the phrase "The sins of the father will be visited down to the third and fourth generation" in the books of Exodus, Deuteronomy and Numbers in the Bible. Though these words are spoken by God as a consequence for disobeying God's commands, I think the writers of these books were simply making a wise observation. The sins of parents are passed on to the children, and if each generation is actively working on healing, then it can get worked out of the family system by the third or fourth generation.

I write all of this to say, as part of loving yourself and getting ready for the love of a lifetime, find a great counselor, invest in learning what your personal craziness is about, and work on it. We all have stuff. You have stuff.

> *The question is, "Will you manage your stuff, or will your stuff manage you?"*

It's your stuff. You may have inherited it from one or both of your parents, or there may have been some traumatic life event that has given you stuff that nobody else has had. Whatever the source of your stuff, it doesn't do you any good to blame your parents or life or God or to bemoan that "It isn't fair." You are right. It's not fair. Now what? It's still your stuff. It will always be your stuff. The question is, "Will you manage your stuff, or will your stuff manage you?"

If we don't know what our issues are, they will manage us. If we know what our problems are but we don't work on them, they will manage us. Being managed by our "stuff"— our problems and issues—will either prevent or get in the way of finding and keeping the love of a lifetime. Why? Because whenever our partners hit those tender spots, we are going to react and blame them for our stuff, which is both unfair and really confusing. Furthermore, if you don't deal with your weak areas, you doom yourself to making the same mistakes over and over again.

## Predictable Patterns

One of my good buddies has been married twice. The first was to a stripper, whom he started dating soon after he started watching her in a club. If I remember correctly, he left that relationship for another woman, whom he married soon after his divorce was final. I knew him when things started to go south in his second marriage. We had conversations about how he was frustrated in the relationship and thinking he might want someone else. I encouraged him to get some counseling, either for just him or for him and his wife. Instead, he had an affair with one of the servers in the Moose Club we were part of. While he was clearly physically attracted to her, he wasn't that excited about her as a person. Eventually, his wife figured out he was having an affair. He left evidence that was easy for her to find. I don't think this was conscious. I think unconsciously he wanted to get caught. He is a very bright guy and knew how to cover his tracks if he wanted to. His wife became understandably very upset and left him. When I last talked to him, he was still deeply involved in his relationship with the server. My guess would be that he married her, eventually became unhappy in that marriage, had another affair, divorced again, etc. It is a pattern in his life that is predictable and will be until he sits down and figures out what the stuff is that is managing his behavior in his relationships.

My guess is you have people in your life who are clearly being managed by their issues—friends who leave an alcoholic or abusive relationship, only to find themselves with an alcoholic or abuser in the next relationship. This is what I mean by our stuff managing us unless we work to figure out how to manage it.

## Mommy Issues

Here's a different angle on how our past affects us and our relationships. Whenever I leave my mom, it's almost impossible to get out the door. She has an unending list of things she wants me to remember and things she wants to talk to me about before I leave. From the second I say, "Good-bye, Mom," the verbal flood begins. "Oh, wait! Remember ...! And there's ...! Did you ...?" This continues nonstop as I walk out the door and as I'm trying to get in the car. I have stood at the open door, trying to get into my car and leave for fifteen minutes before Mom finally stops. It drives me nuts! This has happened as far back as I can remember. So now, if I'm leaving for work or something, and I've kissed my wife good-bye and, as I'm walking out the door she says, "Wait! Remember ..." what do you think happens? All those feelings of impatience and anger at my mom start flooding back and get directed at Winter.

Winter is not my mom. It is unfair for me to take out on Winter my issues with my mother. Yet, those feelings are there for me. If I did not know that this was my stuff and where it came from, I guarantee I would get very impatient with Winter and eventually act in some way that would be really inappropriate and hurt Winter's feelings—because my baggage was managing me.

## Getting Help

It's also a lot easier to know what somebody else's problem is than to know our own. This is one of the reasons a good counselor is helpful. He or she can help us identify our behavior patterns, gain some knowledge of their source, and give us ways of dealing with and managing them. We can also ask our partners to help us by telling them, "This is my quirk. Can you help me by treading gently around my quirk?" It's very helpful for our partners to know, for instance, what our weird fear is, so when we are talking about that great clown exhibition we went to and suddenly we're curled up in a corner, hugging our pillow and sucking our thumbs, our partners can remember, "Oh yeah! You've got clown stuff. I am going to tread carefully because I know this is a tender spot for you." Remember—this is our stuff. It is not our partners' job to fix us. It is not our partners' fault that we have stuff. They can help, but it's not their responsibility. It's ours.

Here's the very cool thing. If Doctor Hendrix is right, that we marry or form long-term partnerships with a partner for what they represent that is unresolved in our family of origin, if we can work through our problems together and love each other through it, we can give each

*if we can work through our problems together and love each other through it, we can give each other one of the most amazing gifts in life: deep, long-lasting healing and redemption.*

other one of the most amazing gifts in life: deep, long-lasting healing and redemption. That, my dear reader, is something that cannot be bought or sold. This is one of the ultimate promises and gifts of the love of a lifetime.

## Exercise 4: Personal and Family "Stuff" Discovery

Sit down with a big piece of paper and write down all the family members you can think of, as far back as you can go. Diagram how they are all related, connected, and what the relationships are like. Are they close? Are they too close/ enmeshed? Are they disconnected? Is there abuse in some of them? What kind? Are there uncles or aunts nobody talks about? Why? What family stories do you know? Write it all down.

What holes are there in your knowledge? Why doesn't Grandpa talk to Aunt Flo anymore? Get on the phone, or at the next family meal, ask family members who might know to fill in the gaps. If you don't feel like you can ask those questions, why not? What would happen if you did? All families have things they don't talk about. Try asking the questions. See what happens.

After you have your family mapped out, ask yourself how these relationships and family dynamics have affected you. This is a good beginning to explore your stuff. You can pack this up and take it to your therapist to discuss further. He or she will be amazed at how proactive you are.

**Winter's reflections:** Family—you can't live with them and you don't want to live without them! I love my parents and my family of origin, but we have not always had easy relationships. There was a time when family gatherings were just painful for me. I was trying to sort out my "stuff," and my family kept unintentionally poking my weak spots. I needed a way to stay connected without becoming enmeshed. I had to figure out a different way to interact with them. I decided to view each visit as an anthropological study. I simply observed anything that hit a nerve for me. I mentally watched and took notes. I had a few key phrases I employed anytime I felt anxious when I was with them. If you could have read my mind, you likely would have heard, *Curious. So that's how this tribe operates*, or *Interesting, that seems to run counter to the family's sense of well-being.* Sounds crazy, but it helped. Whether you are dealing with extended family, children, or your spouse, find ways to remain connected as you sort out your stuff.

# Chapter 4

## Finding the Love of a Lifetime

*The best advice my father gave me was, "Marry your best friend."*

The best advice my father gave me was, "Marry your best friend." What he didn't say was, "There is a vast, qualitative difference between very, very good and best." When we are with our best friends, the two basic foundational building blocks of a long-term, committed relationship are easy. These are communication and trust. Communication with our best friends is effortless. That's why they are our best friends! We share interests, jokes, advice, movies, thoughts, stories, music, and the vast majority of life. It's fun; it's easy. They are our confidants, primary advisors, playmates, and support systems all wrapped up in one. This is why "best friend" is synonymous with "soul mate." We trust our best friends with the best and worst of us because we know they will always have our backs. When the chips are down, where do we go? Our best friends. When we get new jobs or a raise, who are the first people we call? Our best friends. Our dog dies, who do we call? Our best friends. Marry your best friend, and you have got the world's best TastyKake. (Everybody who grew up on the East Coast in the '70s knows that "TastyKake is all the good things, all the good things wrapped up in one.")

I'm not saying that you can't marry a very, very good friend and be happy. It just takes more work. When people say, "Marriage takes a lot of hard work," I think this is what they're talking about. Honestly, I don't think Winter and I feel like we work hard at our marriage. I certainly don't. This is not to say there haven't been things that have been hard or challenging to work through. Most of the time, it's easy and good and a heck of a lot of fun. We don't fight. We do from time to time disagree, or one might hurt the other by accident, but we talk about it and work through it together because we have really, really solid *communication and trust*. Communication and trust: easy with our best friends; sometimes hard work with someone else.

## The Quest

So, how do we find this mythical beast, "the love of a lifetime"? It is a great quest, greater than any Holy Grail sought by knights of legend. I was driving one afternoon with a group of youths from our church's youth group. We were talking about this question: "How do you find the right guy?" (The lone male youth was asleep in the back seat; it had been a long day.) I said, "You want the truth? It's a numbers game." Some people are lucky, and they don't have to date a lot of people to find the right one, but for most, you have to meet and talk to a lot of possibilities. There are just not many people who fall into the "best friend" category. There is also the complicating factor of whether or not they fit the bill of falling into the right gender category that we want to have a romantic relationship with and not just a friendship.

We know very quickly when we meet someone who might be a best friend. They're easy to talk to. We have a lot of similar tastes and values. Maybe we have different ones, but we love talking about those similarities and differences. We just "click." We love hanging out with them and being around them because they make life fun. For most of us, these people are few and far between. That's one of the things that what makes them *best*.

Hopefully, we will also find one or two or maybe even a few best friends who have no romantic possibility because they are not in the right gender category for us. These are invaluable friends who are worth staying in touch with—because everybody needs good friends they are not romantically involved with.

Hopefully, we will eventually find the one best friend we want to share all of life with, the love of a lifetime.

## Ways to Search

**Old School**: How do you get to know new people? Networking. Where are all the places you naturally meet people? Work, family events, faith community, hobbies, school. Talk to members of the gender that fits your target romantic group with no other agenda than getting to know them. Winter and I combined at least two of the above categories. We met through work, which also happened to be our faith communities. She was the church administrator at the church where I had to go through a portion of the long, arduous hazing process known as "ordination" in the United Methodist Church. She was fun, beautiful, clever, and a wicked teaser. Yep, we had it firing on all cylinders!

**How People Roll Today**: More and more of the people I marry are meeting through online dating sites. Having never used one, they appear to me to be a heck of a lot better than the old want ads in the newspaper. You get to have a personal profile, which is basically a long, drawn-out advertisement for you. Then you get to troll other people's "Why I love me and you should too" ads to see who might be of interest. With the right site, it's a way of getting to know a little bit about a lot of people in a short period of time, and you can discover significant parts of somebody's personality, interests, hobbies, etc. without the pressure of potential physical contact. To put it another way, a dating site is a means to get to know somebody without sex getting in the way—which leads us to the challenge of sex.

## The Sex Conundrum

♪ Salt-N-Pepa, "Let's Talk About Sex"

To wait or not to wait, that is the question. Whether 'tis nobler to suffer the slings and arrows of suppressed desire until marriage or to cast off restraint and sail into the winds of fortune, this decision is no joke. As a society, we have put our young adults in an impossible situation. We are physically ready to have sex and start bearing children somewhere between the ages of twelve and seventeen years old. Disturbingly, as we introduce all kinds of hormones into our bodies through the critters we eat and the things we drink, the age of physical sexual maturity is getting younger by the year.[1] At the same time, we have greatly expanded the time we spend in adolescence. It is a common experience for young adults to leave home, go to college or start to work, and return home. Because of all kinds of social and economic factors, it is tough to break free. For example, we cannot get a student loan for college without including our parents' financial information until after we are twenty-six years old, even if we have been living on our own and taking care of ourselves for years. It is quite challenging for anyone to have started a career, have his own home, and be an independent adult much before thirty years of age. To top it off, we have faith communities that insist sex outside of marriage is a dire sin, and the only appropriate thing to do is to wait until you get married. What is a boy or girl to do?

## Treat Sex with the Respect It Deserves

While most people come to the conclusion that it is an unrealistic expectation to wait for marriage to have sex, our faith communities have a point. Sex is powerful, powerful stuff. It's not something to be entered into lightly, and if entered into lightly and casually, it's often very confusing and potentially deeply damaging to everyone involved.

---

[1] For more info see: "Early Puberty for Girls", by Kathleen O'Grady, Canadian Women's Health Network's Network Magazine, Issue 11, No 1, Fall/Winter 2009. Available on-line at http://www.cwhn.ca/network-reseau/11-1/11-1pg4.html. - See more at: https://nwhn.org/early-puberty-for-girls-the-new-normal-and-why-we-need-to-be-concerned/#sthash.0w8u5gG8.dpuf

In my opinion, the hook-up culture of casual sex without any care for or necessarily even knowing your partner is evil. "Evil? Isn't that a bit strong?" you might ask. I would argue that most of the challenges we have as humankind— war, genocide, in- fanticide, famine, global warming, you name it—can

> *Sex is powerful, powerful stuff. It's not something to be entered into lightly, and if entered into lightly and casually, it's often very confusing and potentially deeply damaging to everyone involved.*

be traced back to two basic challenges of the human condition: self-centeredness ("I am the only thing that matters") and objectification ("You are not fully human; therefore I can do to you whatever I want.")

## Self-Centeredness and Objectification

You can see how self-centeredness and objectification play out in a wide variety of places in our lives:

1) In war, every enemy gets their own special nick-name. In WWII, Germans were "Krauts" and the Japanese were "Japs." In the Korean and Vietnam wars, the enemy were "Gooks." In the first and second Gulf War, the enemy were "Ragheads." Why do we do this? For the vast majority of people, it's really hard to kill another human being. In fact, Brigadier General S.L.A. Marshall found that only 15 to 20 percent of men on average in WWII would "take any part with their weapons" when the moment of

truth came in combat. Modern armies have to go to great psychological lengths in order to desensitize and condition their soldiers to kill.[2] This desensitization has always begun with making the enemy into an object, something less than human and therefore easier to kill.

2) In the way people are objectified in advertising and popular culture, especially women.

3) In the way we treat the environment and the rest of life on the planet, demanding that we get to exploit life for our purpose and profit with no thought to the consequences or replenishing.

The list goes on and on. At the root of most, if not all, human-caused tragedy, at the root of all evil, is one or both of these factors, self-centeredness and objectification. You cannot engage in truly casual sex without making your partner into "an object of desire" whose primary, if not sole, purpose at that moment is your self-gratification. Emily Esfahani Smith writes, "Hooking up, in fact, shares the defining feature of a sexual assault: using another person for your own sexual gratification, without any regard as to what that person wants or how he or she feels" [3] Evil.

---

[2] For more info see: Lt. Col. Grossman, Dave, June 1, 2007, "Hope on the Battlefield" retrieved from http://greatergood.berkeley.edu/article/item/hope_on_the_battlefield

[3] Smith, Emily Esfhahani, November 5, 2012, "A Plan to Reboot Dating" retrieved from https://www.theatlantic.com/sexes/archive/2012/11/a-plan-to-reboot-dating/264184/

## The Challenge with Casual Sex

Casual sex, even when mutually agreed upon and not a one-night stand, tends to get confusing. Two of my friends in Florida had a long-term "friends with benefits" relationship. Let's call them Fred and Wilma. Wilma had a long-term boyfriend, Joe, who lived in another state, many hours' drive away. Everybody was on the same page together. Wilma was deeply committed to Joe, but because they lived so far from each other, they had an open relationship, free to date and have relationships with other people. Fred knew this was the deal when he and Wilma began their relationship together. Wilma was very up front, honest, and open with him and with Joe. Fred and Wilma lived together happily for a while. Whenever Joe came to town to visit, Wilma was with Joe, but over time, this became very confusing, especially for Fred. Fred felt understandably hurt, angry, and jealous when Joe came to town, and he and Wilma went off together. Fred eventually ended the relationship.

So, instead of resorting to casual sex, do you get married very young because you don't want to wait for sex, in the full knowledge that neither of you is really ready for that type of commitment? Or do you have sex before you are ready to make a long-term commitment and find that you have overcommitted to a partner who you're not sure you want to be committed to? I know people who have made the decision to get married young because they wanted to have sex, and I know people who have made the decision to marry because they had been having sex and were overcommitted. All of them felt like this was a mistake. This is the sex conundrum, to which there are no easy answers.

## Being in "Control"?

The *New York Times* has published a number of essays on love and sex from their "Modern Love College" essay contest. "After a First Time, Many Second Thoughts" shows clearly how difficult it is to navigate the sexually charged troubled waters of our times. In the article, Arla describes her first time. She believed that losing her virginity would empower her, freeing her from the confines of a restrictive religious community and belief system in which she had been raised. She would finally be liberated. Arla met a guy she liked but didn't want to have as a long-term lover. She asked him to be her first time because it was important for her to be in control. Arla believed, "if I did everything right, I could control the emotions involved in physical intimacy." After their night together, she attempted to remain connected as friends, but Zach was not interested. Arla was angry because she felt used, until she realized she had used him. She concludes her article by writing, "I thought losing my virginity would liberate me, and in a sense it did. I learned that no matter how calculating I am—right guy, right time, right place—I can't control other people's feelings, or even my own. And there's a strange freedom in that knowledge. It allowed me to let go." [4]

## Sex Is Not Casual

When I struggle with how to answer deep, challenging life questions, the first place I go to is my faith. The phrase, "A man leaves his father and mother, clings to his wife and

---

[4] Knudson, Arla, May 28, 2015, "After a First Time, Many Second Thoughts", retrieved from https://www.nytimes.com/2015/05/31/style/after-a-first-time-many-second-thoughts.html?_r=1

they become one flesh" [5]is repeated over and over in the Old and New Testament. This really is a fitting description of what sex does. When we are naked and intimate with each other, we are at our most vulnerable, most trusting, most revealing of ourselves. With sex, we get to know each other inside and out—literally. Sex creates oneness, a fusion of body, mind, and spirit. There is nothing about sex that is a casual thing. Sex is deep, touching on some of the most fragile parts of not only our bodies but our psyches. In order to be this vulnerable with somebody else, you have to have deep trust, which is why sex naturally leads to serious commitment. Given that this is the reality of physical intimacy, you can see why it can get very, very confusing when we go at it casually, without any commitment. Even when you think, *Hey, this is just a casual thing. We've talked about it. We're all on the same page,* more often than not, one or both partners find themselves more emotionally involved than they intended or ever thought they would be, and when the relationship ends, they feel resentful or used or angry or sad or conflicted.

I entered into a relationship with a woman as I was in the process of getting a divorce. The legal paperwork had already been filed, so the marriage was all but over except for the wait time required by the State of Oregon. I knew at the time that this was not the time to get into a serious relationship, because I was well aware that I was an emotional basket case. I was grieving, processing what I had done wrong and what I needed to work on. It was not the right time to have a serious relationship. I communicated

---

[5] Genesis 2:24, Matthew 19:5, Ephesians 5:31, New Revised Standard Version

this very clearly to her. For a couple months, we had a really good time, enjoying each other's company. It was a comfort to me in the midst of a time of deep pain.

Because of the intimacy we shared, both of our feelings started to get really confused. I began to care deeply for her. She was finishing her PhD in economics and had a dream to work for the World Bank. When she began talking about ditching this dream and staying for me, I freaked out because I knew I was not ready for a long-term commitment and did not want her to abandon her dreams for me. So I broke up with her, which was very painful for both of us but especially for her. I still remember the sound of her grief as I closed the door and walked down the hall.

## Nobody Likes to Wait, and Yet ...

Respect and honor the power of sex. I would highly recommend that we choose to wait until we care enough for somebody else that we are ready to make a serious commitment to the relationship. If we aren't ready to make a commitment to marriage itself, then make a commitment to the type of relationship that we are willing to treat like a marriage, because this is the kind of relationship that sex naturally leads to.

What do we do while we wait? It is physically and emotionally challenging to choose to wait until we have found the right person with whom we are ready to have a long-term committed relationship. It is challenging when we are alone and feeling lonely. It is challenging when we have gone out on a date or two and we are feeling really physically attracted to somebody. It is really, really challenging to wait when we are unsure that we are ready to make a commitment, but we have already rounded first and second base and the third-base coach is motioning us to make that run for home plate!

It is worth waiting until we are sure this is a person we want to commit to. Winter and I were in the middle of a garage sale when a guy walked in with a T-shirt on. On the back of the T-shirt was a sexy brunette in red lingerie, long red tail, and horns, with the words, "Hell isn't so bad." Believe me, it does not matter how attractive, alluring, or seductive it looks; hell really is hell. In fact, it is my deepest belief that the devil does not look scary or terrifying. The devil is what looks most attractive and seductive and is what destroys us in the end.

> *Believe me, it does not matter how attractive, alluring, or seductive it looks; hell really is hell. In fact, it is my deepest belief that the devil does not look scary or terrifying. The devil is what looks most attractive and seductive and is what destroys us in the end.*

Waking up in the morning with someone we really don't like as a person or who we quickly realize was a mistake is no fun for anyone. Waking up with someone we really care for and are intensely attracted to but can't have because he or she doesn't want us is a special kind of hell. Fighting, shouting, and throwing things because we can't figure out how to make our relationship work is hell. Divorce is hell. Relationships can have many hells, and jumping into the sack before we're ready can be a wide and paved "highway to hell" that, unlike the AC/DC song, is no fun at all!

## Your Delaying Action

What do we do while we wait? Masturbate! Wait a minute! I feel a song coming on!

> "When you've got to wait, masturbate!
>> It's got rhythm and rhyme!
> When you've got to wait, masturbate!
>> Put some James Brown in it!
> When you've got to wait, masturbate!
>> Get jazzy on it!"

Seriously, choosing to wait is tough, and it is absolutely ridiculous that my faith tradition gives the primary message that we should wait until we get married and provide no alternatives for our sexuality, even implying that masturbation is wrong, sinful, and shameful. You've probably even heard the story (at least if you are Christian) of the grave sin that Onan had of "spilling his seed on the ground." This story has been taken out of context and used by men with serious hang-ups about their sexuality, to say that masturbation is evil. This is stinkin' thinkin'. If we read the "biblical" story, it's clear that the sin was not masturbation. He wasn't even masturbating in the story. He was engaging in the only method of birth control available to people at the time, known as withdrawal. The sin was refusing to impregnate his dead brother's wife so that his brother might have children through him. (It's a weird story to begin with, but to briefly explain what was going on: the story deals with the laws of inheritance at the time. By refusing to give his brother children, he was essentially stealing from his brother.)

## Love Yourself

Don't buy the hype! You want to be a great lover? How can we do that if we don't know how our own bodies work? Guys, we need to figure out how to delay orgasm long enough for our partners to be there with us. Gals, you need to figure out how your parts work so you can be there with us. Different people have different buttons that need to be pushed in different orders. Great sex starts with knowing ourselves, revealing that to our partners, and working together to achieve a mutual shared goal.

You want to figure out how to wait until you find someone you are ready to make a serious commitment to? Masturbate. When I said "love yourself," I meant that literally. Do it. Feel no shame. Our sexuality is an amazing gift from God and one of the primary needs we have in life. Breathing, food, shelter, clothing, and sex—these are basic needs we all have. It is the way God made us and wired us. Honor God. Honor thyself. Honor thy partner.

There are some great how-to books out there on how to physically be a great lover. Did you know that men and women can have multiple orgasms? Yes! Nirvana exists! There are exercises and things you can do physically to prepare yourself to be a great lover. All of it begins with working on you—literally.

## Partner Selection

*We cannot choose partners thinking we are going to change them!* I had a friend who said, "All women choose the man that they want to marry based on what they want to change in him." I have some sympathy for this. I thought along similar lines when I was much younger: "This is a good person. I see it in them, and if they just stop doing *xyz*, then they can fulfill their potential. My love can show them how good they are." This was and is stinkin' thinkin' on so many levels:

1) It is the height of arrogance and obnoxiousness. We are clearly conveying to our partners that they are not good enough—that we don't love them for who they are but who we think they should be. If we are in a relationship to change somebody, even if we never say it, we communicate it. This runs counter to all of the most basic elements of finding—and keeping—the love of a lifetime. How do we trust someone who is trying to change us? How do we love someone who really doesn't love us? Even if their behavior is self-destructive, we are saying, "You are not good enough for me. I know what's best for you. Stay with me, and I'll fix you. Then, I will love all that is you." That's not love.

2) There are only two people in the universe who can save or change a person: that individual and God. That's why there is the saying that alcoholics or drug addicts have to "hit rock bottom" before they can quit. This is because they have to choose to change. They have to decide for themselves, "This no longer works for me. I don't want it anymore. I am going to change," and more often than not, "I can't change on my own. I need help."

If I am going to change me, I have to recognize that there is something I want to change, and I have to be willing to do the work of changing. It is really, really difficult to change deeply ingrained habits, especially if you are with people who don't support that change. I have come to the conclusion that the best diet for me to eat is a primarily vegetarian diet. When I eat as a vegetarian, I feel better physically and emotionally. It's *so much easier* to maintain a healthy weight for my body. I feel like I am eating in a healthy way for myself and the life around me. It is unequivocally the best choice for me, and yet it is so hard to follow through on as a lifestyle! I live in Iowa, the pork-producing capital of the United States! Meat is everywhere. You can't avoid it if you are going to eat with anybody outside your family. It's often the easiest thing to cook if you're tired and you just want to throw together a meal, and I love the smell, taste, and texture of all things meat. It is hard when you are really hungry at a friend's barbecue and there are hamburgers, hot dogs, pork and beans, and potato chips, to say, "No, I'm just going to eat the potato chips."

This is why it's really important to have healthy boundaries, to be very clear about where we end and other people begin. This is why it's important to know ourselves and love ourselves, so that we know what works for us in life and in relationship and what does not. This works on all levels, from wanting to have a particular lifestyle to not being with somebody who physically abuses us. If you want to have an upper-class lifestyle, don't get involved with an auto mechanic and then expect him to go to college so that he can be an accountant. It's not fair to you, and it's sure as heck not fair to him.

## Know Yourself

We might think, *Oh, that's really shallow. I would never do that.* I cannot tell you the number of people who find themselves in this type of situation, especially if they get into a serious, committed relationship when they are young adults. Would you want to marry a pastor? Or a coach? Or a school

superintendent? I can tell you, it takes a very special partner to put up with all of the physical moving from place to
place that these careers entail, let alone all of the emotional
workplace politics that are more often than not the cause of
the constant moving.

My ex-wife had very clear expectations about what I
would do for a career because it affected her. She was
right—what people do for work has profound effects on
their partners. My career affected how she perceived herself and us in society—our status—and how people looked
at us and thought about us. Having a husband who was
a United Methodist pastor did not fit the image of how
she wanted to portray herself and her family to society. It
was neither prestigious nor honorable—nor intellectual
enough. We were young, and I didn't have complete clarity
on what I wanted to do. I didn't know myself enough to be
able to say, "I am a United Methodist pastor. This is part of
the deal of being with me. If that doesn't work for you, we
might love each other a lot, we might be a great fit for each
other in a lot of ways, but I'm a United Methodist pastor.
You need to be with someone else." This caused great ten-
sion in our relationship. She kept encouraging me to go to
school, get a PhD in something that had real status in our
culture. Definitely not religion. The truth and the fact of
the matter is that being the spouse of a United Methodist
pastor is a commitment all its own. We commit to move at
the beck and call of our bishop. Our lives are not our own,
and the politics of working with churches can be brutal,
not just on the pastor but on every single member of the
family. She had good reason to look on my eventual chosen
profession with great pause. My profession was one of the

reasons we both came to the conclusion that the relationship did not work for either of us.

## Honor Your Needs

If we love somebody a lot but can't understand why they don't treat us right, we need to be able to clearly outline what *treating us right* means and be willing to say, "This is what I need in my committed relationship. If I can't get what I need, I need to be by myself." This is a lot easier to do when we are dating than after we have made a serious commitment. There's not a lot at stake physically or emotionally when we are dating. If we are living together or married, it is a *lot* tougher to say, "This is not working for me," divide up our now-shared stuff, and move away from each other. We should not think that because we love somebody a lot, we can change them or that they will change for us. We need to love our partners for who they are, and if we don't love all of them, all their curves and edges and perfect imperfections, don't punish them and ourselves by getting into a long-term committed relationship with them. It's cruel and unusual punishment—for everyone involved.

If someone is abusive or is abusing drugs or alcohol, we need to be able to define and keep clear boundaries. This means saying things like, "You may not hurt me. It's not okay. If it happens again, I will leave." It also means that, once we draw those lines, we absolutely

> *Saying, "I need xyz in my life in order to be happy" is entirely different from saying, "You need to change xyz about yourself in order for me to be happy."*

follow through on them. If we say we will leave, leave—and don't go back. Period.

Do you see how this is different than trying to change someone? Saying, "I need *xyz* in my life in order to be happy" is entirely different from saying, "You need to change *xyz* about yourself in order for me to be happy."

# Chapter 5

## The Wedding

So, this is it! You have found the love of your lifetime! And, you are ready to make the big leap into the serious, long-term commitment of all serious, long-term commitments, marriage. "Mawage. Mawage is what bwings us togever today. Mawage. That bwessed awangement. The dweam within a dweam!" Sorry, I had a *The Princess Bride* moment. Woo-hoo! Congratulations!

♪ Train, "Marry Me"

This is it! The big one! It doesn't get any bigger than this! Really, it doesn't. Promising to care for somebody un-

> *Mawage. Mawage is what bwings us togever today. Mawage. That bwessed awangement. The dweam within a dweam! –Archbishop in The Princess Bride*

til the day you die, regardless of what comes, is virtually an act of insanity. Think about what life throws at all of us. We have to figure out how to make a living, find sufficient lodging that at least keeps us warm in the winter and cool in the summer, make babies, raise adults, deal with the decline and death of our parents, and eventually our own physical decline and death. Throw in side orders of personal fulfillment, possibly competing careers, and the ups and downs that economies and wars and life throw at all us, and we can see why the best image I have of marriage is standing at the edge of a tall cliff of which you can't see the bottom, holding hands, jumping together, and hoping against all hope that you fly. Welcome to the show!

This is the big kickoff that sets the tone for your life together. What is it going to be about? Is it going about the wedding or the marriage? At this point in my life, I have officiated well over one hundred weddings. Every wedding has a spiritual energy where, after the wedding, there is the feeling of "That was good," "That was bad," or "Meh." There have been a few weddings where I have gone home feeling, "That was really good. I have great hope for that couple." There have been a few where I have gone home feeling, "I will not stop praying for them because, oy, that did not feel good." Most weddings I go home feeling "Meh." Here's the kicker: I have had couples or parents of couples come back to me years later and either say what a great or bad job I did based on whether or not the couple is still together!

Guess what? This is not about me. This is all about you! I'm not going home with you. I'm not part of negotiating who sleeps on which side of the bed. I'm not living your life. I've got my own problems. Whoever is officiating at the ceremony is merely there to facilitate the promise you are making to each other before God and your family and friends.

You make or break it. The people around you may help or hinder. Your pastor or imam or rabbi might have some tools to help you if you get in trouble, but this is your baby!

I do, however, have some recommendations around what I have seen work really well in a wedding that sets the tone for a great marriage and what does not—and makes me want to go home and pray without ceasing, and maybe take a long, hot, sterilizing shower.

## Boomershine's Wedding Do and Don't

Make sure the wedding serves the marriage and not vice versa. I see a lot of people getting really wrapped up in all the "stuff" of a wedding—from T-shirts for the bridal and groomal party (if it's a bridal party, a bridal shower, etc., why isn't it then also a "groomal" party, etc.? Maybe because it just sounds too silly) to matching bags to flowers to not just a rehearsal dinner but an engagement party to a pre-rehearsal party. *The stuff is unending!* People are spending ungodly amounts of money on weddings, too. According to costofawedding.com, the cost of the average wedding is $26,444.

Here is a list of just some of the stuff that can go into making up that cost:

- **Clothing and Accessories**
  - o Wedding Dress
  - o Dress accessories
  - o Tuxedo or suit/rent or purchase

- **Beauty and Spa**
  - o Hair Dresser
  - o Makeup service
  - o Manicure and pedicure

- **Entertainment**
  o DJ and/or
  o Live band and/or
  o Musician(s), soloist, or ensemble

- **Flowers and Decorations**
  o Boutonnieres, corsages
  o Bridal bouquet
  o Bridesmaid bouquets
  o Event decorations
  o Flower arrangements
  o Table centerpieces
  o Flowers for the Flower Girl
  o Petals to be thrown by the Flower Girl

- **Printed Material**
  o Programs
  o Announcements
  o Guest book
  o Invitations and reply cards
  o Postage
  o Reception menus
  o Save-the-date cards
  o Table name/Number and escort/place cards
  o Thank-you cards

- **Gifts and Favors**
  o Gift(s) for attendants
  o Gift(s) for parents
  o Tips (for all services)
  o Wedding favors

- **Jewelry**
  o Engagement ring
  o Wedding rings/ bands

- **Photos & Videos**
  o Digital or photo CD/DVD
  o Engagement session
  o Prints and/or enlargements
  o Wedding album(s) or photo book(s)
  o Wedding photographer/ videographer

- **Wedding Planner**
  o A la carte services
  o Day-of coordinator
  o For getting started
  o Full service
  o Month-of direction

- **Venue, Catering, and Rentals**
  - o Ceremony officiator
  - o Event accessories
  - o Event bar service
  - o Event food service
  - o Event location
  - o Event rentals
  - o Hotel room for after reception
  - o Limo rental
  - o Other transportation
  - o Rehearsal dinner
  - o Wedding cake/dessert

I can guarantee you, for the weddings I perform today, $26,000 is often a low-ball figure.

Now, let's be clear. I'm not saying that if you have the money, it's not worth spending on a great party. *But the party is not what the wedding is about.* The wedding itself is not what the wedding is about. A wedding is about the promise of a lifetime. It is about a marriage.

## Put Some "Skin in the Game"

What if we were to invest as much emotional and physical time planning the marriage as we do the wedding? I have heard the legend of a colleague of mine who charges the couples he marries a donation of 10 percent of the costs of the wedding to his church. "What?" many people ask. Does that sound like a ridiculous cost for a church and a person to preside over a wedding? It did to me at first. My policy has generally been that I am happy to receive whatever donation a couple is willing to give to the church and me

> *What if we were to invest as much emotional and physical time planning the marriage as we do the wedding?*

because I believe that what we are all about is helping to facilitate a relationship with people and God. As I thought about it, I think there is an argument to be had for an investment to be made *in the marriage*. The ceremony itself, the words you speak and the promises you make—that is what the wedding is about. Not the dresses, not the flowers, not the colors or cake or dancing or any of the other stuff around it. If the wedding serves the marriage, maybe it would be appropriate to spend not 10 percent but 51 percent on the church and the pastor. Then you are literally investing more money in what matters than on stuff and fluff.

At any rate, put some "skin in the game" in the marriage when planning a wedding. Invest in the marriage. Do some real premarital work together. Find a great family-systems counselor and spend a few months in getting coached on how to communicate, how to fight well, how to build and reinforce trust over the long run, how to know each other's personal hot buttons, and how to care for each other around those issues.

## Prepare/Enrich Premarital Counseling

"Prepare/Enrich" is one of the best processes I've seen for this, aside from a great family-systems counselor. Prepare/Enrich is "the leading relationship inventory and skill-building program used nationally and internationally ... custom tailored to a couple's relationship and [providing] couple exercises to build their relationship skills." [6]

---

[6] See the homepage of www.prepare-enrich.com

## My Complete Turnaround

When I recommend Prepare/Enrich and/or premarital counseling, you should know this is a complete 360-degree turnaround from my attitude about premarital counseling four years ago. Based on my own experience, I believed for most of my career that premarital counseling did not work. In my first marriage, we were required by the Catholic Church, of which my ex-wife was a member, to do at least six sessions of premarital counseling. We went on an "Engaged Discovery" retreat, where we took a survey of our opinions on all of the issues that we would encounter in a life together: money, children, work, sex, etc. Then we compared them, looking for the places where we agreed and where we differed. We talked about them together and with the priest. This was fine, but we really didn't find out anything we didn't already know. The things we were struggling with we already knew, and the other stuff was just fine. The priest was a nice guy, and we got to know him a little better, but talking together about life's issues with the priest did not raise any red flags, nor did it help with the very real problems we were struggling with, especially those that came later. We were set on getting married, and there was very little that might have changed that.

This is the challenge with required premarital counseling. If it is imposed from the outside on you, then it is just another hoop to jump through to get you to the ultimate goal of being married: caterer—check, wedding cake—check, church and officiant—check. My ex-wife and I jumped through the hoops and were "successfully" married—until we both decided the most caring thing we could do for each other was to not be married seven years later.

## My Rules

When I was thinking I might try the whole marriage thing again if I found a partner who fit my father's original best advice ("Marry your best friend"), I had a whole list of criteria that had to be met before a marriage could take place: 1) Don't date women with children. (I had dated one mother with two kids, and it was weird. She, obviously, had to take their needs into account. We could almost never get together, and when we did, the kids came along. It just did not work for me.) 2) Don't tell anybody you love them until six months after you begin dating. 3) Must date for *at least* one year before proposing. 4) Had to be engaged *at least* one year before getting married. All these rules were an effort to try to protect myself from making the same mistakes again.

I met Winter, who already had two kids. Not an option. But she was so darn fun to talk to and hang around. So, against my better judgment, we started dating—but Winter was different. She protected the kids from even knowing that we were dating for months. Within two weeks, I was saying, "I really dig your company," following rule number two. (After we got married, she told me that when I was saying this to her, she was tracing on my back, "I love you, too" with her finger.) Four months later, I asked her to marry me, and nine months after we started dating, we got married. No premarital counseling; all my rules out the window, and we have been really, really happy.

This is why I believed that premarital counseling was a waste of time. First *failed* marriage—lots of premarital counseling and preparation. Second *wildly successful* marriage—no premarital counseling and preparation. Conclusion: if you marry your best friend, who needs preparation? If you don't marry your best friend, all the preparation in the world may not be prophylactic. So, for years, my premarital counseling consisted of forty-five minutes of the best advice I have from one very successful and one failed marriage—until my supervising committee in Oskaloosa, Iowa, wanted me to offer something more.

I went to Prepare/Enrich training reluctantly. To my utter surprise, I found that it was not primarily talking about different life issues that couples might have. Instead, Prepare/Enrich gives exercises on communication, conflict resolution, and listening that couples practice together with a coach. The couples then take that material home, so they have the exercises. This can help them remember how they work, so they have the means to work through challenges together. This is a worthy investment of time, energy, and money. I was pleasantly and thoroughly surprised, and now I offer my couples the options of my best advice or Prepare/Enrich.

## A Question of Priorities

Frankly, whoever guides couples through that process should charge at least $100 to $150 per session, four to six sessions of an hour and a half each. This is the low end of the going rate for a professional counselor. Rates vary widely according to experience and area of the country. I can't tell you the number of people and churches that complain to me about how expensive $600 to $900 is for premarital counseling. If you are spending $26,000 on a wedding, $600 to $900 is a drop in the bucket! Is your marriage worth the investment, or is it all about a big party?

To be very blunt, what is the priority, one night that is

all about a party or hopefully thousands of nights together with the love of a lifetime? Trust me, a little bit of time and money invested up front, if it helps work through the tough times, is worth *a hell of a lot more* than those few hours of time and less than $1,000! Anybody who has been through a divorce could tell you that, if that's all it took to avoid divorce, it would have been time and money well spent. In a divorce, you lose half of everything. Half. Half of all your stuff, your money, and sometimes your retirement. Then, maybe you get to walk away. Unless you have kids. Then there's no walking away—ever. A few hours and less than $1,000 v. half. Add to that ripping out your heart and stomping on it—repeatedly. That's a pretty stark cost-to-benefit ratio in my book. Others would call it a no-brainer.

Granted, counseling or Prepare/ Enrich or something like it is no guarantee. Staying married today in our culture and society can be very

> *In a divorce, you lose half of everything. Half. Half of all your stuff, your money, and sometimes your retirement. Then, maybe you get to walk away.*

challenging, but investing close to nothing in the marriage and being all in for the wedding?

## Boomershine's Best Advice

My best advice again is make sure the wedding serves the marriage and not vice versa. Do everything you possibly can to focus on your partner and make the promise of a lifetime together.

How do we do this when there's all of the craziness of

logistics and coordination of a wedding going on, not to mention the anxiety and suggestions, expectations and requirements of our family and friends? Weddings tend to bring the crazy out of our families about as much as, and sometimes even more than, funerals.

Here's some of my other best advice:

1) **Tell your parents, especially your mom, that one of the best gifts they can give to you is to let your wedding be *your* wedding**. Advice when asked for is appreciated, but the decisions are yours. If your parents are paying for the wedding and believe that because it's their money, they should get to make the decisions, say, "Thanks, but no thanks. This is about me and my partner. If the gift of the wedding comes with strings attached, then we'll do something a lot smaller that is ours." If they are paying for it, they should also be clear on the budget—and it's your job to *stay within the budget.*

2) **Distinguish between wants and needs.** This is a good time to start figuring out the difference between what you want and what you need. You need a partner to get married. You need somebody to officiate and sign the wedding certificate. You need one or two witnesses. You need some kind of location where this will take place. Everything else is a want.

3) **Find someone you trust who is a detail person and will have your agenda in mind, not their own, and ask them to help you make sure that everything you have chosen to happen on the wedding day happens.** If he or she does the worrying about calling and coordinating the cake and the chairs and the music and, and, and, that will go a long way toward being able to focus on your partner and not the details.

4) **Find a faith community and pastor/imam/rabbi or someone who really speaks to you and who you are together as a couple.** Connect with them. Have them help guide you through this process, and stay connected afterward. There's nothing better than good religion, and there's nothing worse than bad religion. Good religion, leaders, faith, and a faith community really helps guide and support you through all the good, bad, and ugly in life. There are a lot of bad or marginal religious communities and leaders out there. There are a few diamonds in the rough. It is worth the quest.

Here are some things to avoid like the plague when planning and carrying out a wedding:

1) **It is not the bride's wedding!** I hear, "It's her day," from brides and grooms and parents all the time. If it's all about her, if it's only her day, if all the wedding is about is making sure that she has her "Cinderella moment," we have missed the entire boat of what a wedding is about, we have sold out entirely to the cultural expectations around us, and we might as well flip a coin. Will it last or not? Heads or tails? Because that's what our culture supports and gives, 50/50. Half of the marriages fail in the United States today. Maybe one reason for this is because if it's all about the bride and making sure she has all the things that are important for a good wedding, then couples are setting themselves up to fail because all they have invested in is a good party. Good luck.

I may be exaggerating a little for effect, but please! If the wedding is about the marriage, if it's about making the promise of a lifetime, then *it takes two.* It's about you both. It's about what is most important to you both! The music, the colors, all the preparations should be about what has most meaning to you both. If it's not meaningful *to the marriage*, don't do it!

2) **Bachelor/bachelorette parties**. There's nothing wrong with getting together with your buddies the night before the wedding for some support. If you are about to make the promise and commitment of a lifetime and you are really thinking about what that means, you probably should feel a little bit anxious, but:

a) Getting so drunk that it affects you the next day is a bad condition to be in when making the promise of a lifetime.

b) Strippers and prostitutes—do you really want to start your marriage with an act that runs completely counter to the commitment you're making? I'm guessing you've been in a committed relationship with your partner for some time before you even got engaged. If you think this is your "last chance to be with someone else," your head is in a very tight, very dark place full of noxious fumes. If you still want to have the opportunity to be with other people, name it, claim it, and call off the wedding now! You have not found the love of a lifetime, nor are you ready to make the promise of a lifetime. You will save yourself and your partner a lot of pain and grief, even if it's on the night before or the day of the wedding.

> *If you think this is your "last chance to be with someone else," your head is in a very tight, very dark place full of noxious fumes. If you still want to have the opportunity to be with other people, name it, claim it, and call off the wedding now!*

c) **Don't come to the wedding ceremony drunk or even tipsy.** If you need to self-medicate before making your vows, there are probably some issues, in the relationship or personally or both, that you need to look at before getting married.

## The Tale of Two Weddings

My first wedding in Ecuador to my now ex-wife was a cliffhanger "fairy tale" wedding. Cliffhanger because the hoops you have to jump through to get married in Ecuador are *unbelievable*. The wedding was in July. We got there in June to make sure there was plenty of time to get all the governmental and church processes accomplished. It was not enough time. We spent countless days running from government official to church official, crisscrossing Quito in a seemingly endless quest to get the right guy in the right office to give us the right piece of paper so we could get married. We didn't know until two days before the wedding whether we would actually be able to get married. What I do know is that, in order to get the Monsignor, the local district church official, to sign off on the wedding, a significant "donation" (i.e., bribe) had to be made to him!

## Let's Call the Whole Thing Off

Talk about stress! The night before the wedding, she and I had a massive fight over issues in our relationship that remained unresolved, to the point that I said, "Maybe we shouldn't do this." I was not making some idle threat or trying to coerce her to coming over to my view. I was serious. In another country, literally thousands of miles away from home, living in her parents' house with relatives who had traveled thousands of miles and friends and family coming from across the country, I seriously suggested calling it off the night before. But, for all the aforementioned reasons, it was too late. The ball that had been rolling had so much weight, there was so much at stake for so many people that calling off the wedding was not something I could follow through on. So, the next morning, as I stood in my tuxedo, getting ready to head out the door, I needed a strong, stiff shot of Johnny Walker's Black Label.

With all we went through and did to each other over seven years of trying to make our marriage work and the divorce, it would have been better to have called off the wedding that night. Remember—we had one of the gentlest, easiest divorces I have ever heard of. In spite of how awful it would have been with all the time, money, and effort so many people had spent to get us to that point, in spite of the incredible embarrassment and extreme awkwardness of leaving my former parents-in-law's house to figure out how to get on a plane home early from Ecuador, it would have been better to have named it, claimed it, and stopped it that night.

The wedding itself was beautiful and all that anybody could hope or dream a wedding would be. It wasn't quite royalty, but it was close. We had the tall, gothic Catholic church, a caring priest, hundreds of family and friends from around the world—and the reception was off the chain! The food was amazing, the cake was fantastic, and we danced until well after midnight. The night ended with a room in the nicest hotel in all of Quito, the capital city of Ecuador. But the wedding was like most wedding cakes—it was really pretty and really sweet but not much else, because we had a broken relationship. According to the standards of what weddings are "supposed to be" in our culture, my first wedding was tops, but the marriage was not good.

## K.I.S.S. (Keep It Simple, Stupid)

My second wedding to Winter is one of the favorite weddings I have ever been to. It was about as simple as a wedding could be. We both worked at South Reno United Methodist Church, and the presiding pastor, John, was our friend, colleague, and boss. We had our place and our officiant. I suggested to John that we get married on Easter after the four packed worship services we had to do that day. He told me I was insane. So we got married on Monday, the day after Easter, April 16, 2001—the day everybody's taxes were due. (Hey, it makes remembering our anniversary easy!) The sanctuary was decorated with all the flowers from Easter. We lived in a small townhouse in a community that had a homeowners' association with a pool and clubhouse. We had the reception at the clubhouse. We bought all the food from Costco, and our friends cooked it and laid it out for us. One of the members of our church owned a brewery in Sparks, so we got a keg of their "Icky Beer," a lovely IPA, and a keg of their root beer for the kids.

When we looked at wedding cakes, we were *stunned* at how expensive they were! We couldn't find a cake we actually wanted to eat for less than $800—and the cake was small! One day as we were walking through Costco, I asked, "What are we going to do about the cake?"

Winter said, "I don't even like wedding cake, do you?"

I said, "Not really."

Winter asked, "So why do we want to spend all that money for something we don't even like?"

At that point I asked, "Well, what is your favorite cake? If you could have any cake to eat in the world, what's your favorite?"

She said, "Cheesecake."

I said, "Costco makes one of the best cheesecakes I have had outside New York City. What if we just do that?"

That's what we did: Costco cheesecake. Not particularly pretty but exactly what we wanted. It was delicious!

Winter found a wedding dress that was beautiful off the rack for a couple hundred dollars. We splurged on one thing: the photographer and pictures, our big expense to the tune of about $800. Our best man and maid of honor were our kids. (I got to adopt Winter's children, Mario and Nina, two short months after we were married.) The whole wedding cost us about $3,000 and it was *so good*.

It started at eleven seventeen sharp! (Given that every wedding starts late and people get all stressed about it, we figured we'd just name it, claim it, and get on with it—11:17 a.m. The perfect time for a wedding!) I was generally relaxed, happy, and content. No need for any alcohol, because I knew I was about to marry my best friend, the love of my lifetime, and life was good! There was a little stress as we were heading to the church because my mom was doing her mom thing, preventing us from leaving the house because we might "forget something." (See, I told you: manage your stuff, or your stuff will manage you.) But, all in all, it was my favorite wedding of all time.

Our wedding was about as simple as simple could be, and it was wonderful! We had the people in attendance who were meaningful to us in our lives—our friends and family. We were at the church we met in, had food we loved to eat, and have great pictures to remember it all—everything that had substance, depth, and meaning in our lives together. We made sure our wedding focused on our marriage.

Winter's two cents: For the record, I wanted to elope. Thomas wanted his loved ones at our wedding. I did it his way because the wedding part of our marriage was more important to him than it was to me. Sometimes it is okay to just let your partner have it their way. (And he was right, it was meaningful to have our loved ones present. Don't tell him I said that.)

# Chapter 6

# Keeping the Love of a Lifetime

You have arrived! You've found the love of a lifetime; married your best friend. Nothing but happily ever after from here on out, right? Well, even if you are solid in your relationship together, life can throw some pretty gnarly curveballs at you that affect you and your relationship together. This is known as stress.

In 1967, Thomas Holmes and Richard Rahe developed a survey to help people identify how much stress they are experiencing in their lives. They placed life events on a scale from one to one hundred. At the top of the scale, the death of a spouse rates one hundred. Toward the bottom of the scale, Christmas rates twelve. The way the survey works, you check every event that you are currently experiencing in your life, add up all the numbers and get a total. If your score is 11 to 150, you have a very small chance of becoming physically or mentally ill in the near future. If your score is between three hundred and six hundred, you have a high or very high risk of becoming physically or mentally ill in the near future. The scale is not perfect. I know many people would rate Christmas a lot more stressful than a twelve! But it does help assess the amount of stress a person is enduring at a particular time in life. (Check out http://www.stress.org/holmes-rahe-stress-inventory/ if you want to take the survey.)

There have been very few years in our lives together when Winter and I haven't had a moderate to high risk of becoming ill in the near future. We have moved a lot, had our daughter Ella, almost lost Winter to an antibiotic-resistant staph infection, wrestled with chronic pain, lost both of Winter's parents, and had very high stress work. According to the stress scale, it is a miracle that all of us haven't been reduced to being curled up in balls, sucking our thumbs in rubber rooms. For a lot of couples, this kind of stress would lead to the end of their relationship. I know that in my first marriage, we would have taken it out on each other.

## Communication and Trust

That has not been the case for Winter and me. In fact, I think it is our relationship that has carried us through the very challenging life we have lived together. Why? Why does stress exacerbate some couples' challenges and strengthen others? I believe the answers to this question are the key to keeping the love of a lifetime.

Remember how I began this book? There are two elements critical to any relationship: communication and trust. Now that you have found the love of your life, now that you have made the commitment of a lifetime, *now* is when the rubber hits the road. (And you thought it was all those sessions in the back seat of your car. Silly you!) It is when you are trying to keep the love of a lifetime that communication and trust share the limelight.

How do you have mind-blowing, toe-curling sex together? How do you work through the tough stuff when all around you is uproar and turmoil? How do you fight? How do you discuss sharing daily chores? How do you negotiate competing needs, wants, and careers? Communication and trust.

## Team Mentality v. Battle of the Sexes

I can't tell you the number of couples I meet, counsel, or hang out with who clearly see their spouse as somebody with whom they are competing. Winter and I have both have conversations with friends of the same gender when they are bad-mouthing their spouse with the clear thought that this is how everybody else's relationships work. My friends will sometimes talk about how they can't go and hang out with the boys or how they're always being nagged by their wives to do this or do that. I always say, "I'm sorry for you. That's not how it is with Winter and me."

**Winter's pet peeve:** I can't stand conversations that begin with "Men always …" or "Women are so …" Your partner is an individual. So are you. To imply that half of the population shares a particular characteristic is ridiculous and insulting. Statements like this are harmful to your partner, to you, and to your relationship. Just imagine how your sons and daughters feel when you let loose with one of these. Dads, do you really want to communicate disdain for females if you have a daughter? Moms, how do you raise kind, honorable sons if you're bashing men?

It is challenging figuring out how to live together. A "battle of the sexes mentality" seems ultimately doomed to end in lose-lose. Jesus once said, "Whenever two or more gather in my name, I am present." I say, "Whenever two or more gather together, there are politics (not the voting kind but the relationship kind). Maybe that's why Jesus needs to be present." What we call politics is the process of how we negotiate sharing limited resources—who gets what and by what means. There are healthy ways of going about doing this, and there are unhealthy ways. Is power shared in the relationship, or is power coercive? Is it a process of mutual negotiation, or does one win at the expense of the other?

I have often heard it said that you have to compromise in a relationship. I say, "Never compromise, or only compromise as an absolute last resort." When we compromise, we both lose. At some level, we both also win. You would think that we would focus on the win, but that's not really how it feels. "Yeah, I won this bit, but overall, I lost." That's how compromise feels.

Compromise is like a blended worship service in a church. In churches today, you have people who really like traditional, classical music with an organ and choir. There aren't a whole lot of people left in the United States who like organ music and classical music. Apparently, one of the last bastions where they can experience this music is in churches, and they are passionate about their music! The vast majority of music listeners prefer listening to some form of popular music, and if they show up for worship, that's often what they want to experience. (I actually like both) For most of my twenty-plus-year career as a pastor, there have been worship wars. Are we going to sing contemporary or traditional music? Some churches have tried to have both types of music in one worship service, thus "blending" the service. You would think that this would be a great idea. There's something for everyone! But, for the most part, what blended worship does is give everyone something to be unhappy about. That's compromise.

Instead of compromise, I suggest we always go for, always work hard for, and always keep working until we can find the win-win. (If you are a fan of Stephen Covey, you will note that we are on Habit #4 of the "Seven Habits of Highly Effective People.") In order to get to win-win, we have to be able to distinguish need from want. Win-win does not mean we get everything we want. It does mean everybody gets what they most need. In fact, sometimes our partner's win can be our win. Let me tell a story to draw a clear picture of what I mean.

*always go for, always work hard for, and always keep working until we can find the win-win*

## The Tale of Two Marriages

When we are talking about the battle of the sexes, nothing seems to illustrate the fight better than the toilet seat. You know what I'm talking about, because if you have ever lived with a member of the opposite sex, you have had this negotiation: "Can the toilet seat be left up, or does it need to be left down at all times? In my first marriage, we fought about the toilet seat! She said, "It is wrong to leave the toilet seat up." I said, "The toilet seat is an object without moral value. It goes up. It goes down." We argued incessantly about the toilet seat. What were we really arguing about? Who was going to win and who was going to lose? Who gets control and who doesn't? Neither of us was willing to lose or cede control. What we were wrestling over was power. When we fight over who is going to win and who is going to lose, when we get into power struggles, everybody loses. In seven years of marriage, I don't recall the issue of the toilet seat ever being resolved, which was a metaphor for our entire relationship. We were constantly engaged in win-lose, zero-sum-game battles. In the end, we lost each other. Lose-lose.

Marriage #2. Winter says to me, "Let me draw you a picture. It's three o'clock in the morning. I'm more than half asleep. I get up to go to the bathroom, and I 'splash down.' Can you imagine how nasty it is to be fully awoken at three in the morning because you have fallen into the toilet? Could you, for me, leave the toilet seat down?"

My response? "Oh, my Lord! That's awful! I am so sorry. I don't want that to happen to you. Of course I will leave the toilet seat down!" It has never been an issue since. The toilet seat in our house from that day on has sat in the downward position, unless we have guests.

## Wants v. Needs

There are some very important principles to glean from these two case studies. The way Winter framed our discussion was not around who was right and who was wrong. She approached me from a place of true, sincere need: "splash-down avoidance." Could she remember to check to see if the toilet seat is up? Of course she could. Is she likely to remember that when she is mostly asleep? Highly doubtful. Is it any skin off of my nose to leave the toilet seat down? Nope. A slight (if any) inconvenience for me; a sincere need for her. This was a no-brainer—unless I chose to go to win/lose, trying to wrest control and power in the relationship. I know, win/lose equals *lose* for everyone. In this case, her win was my win.

Everything we want is not everything we need. No couple needs a five-bedroom house with two or three bathrooms so that they can have a "man cave," a hobby room, and a guest room. We may really, really want these things and have good very reasons for these desires, but they are not needs.

> *Everything we want is not everything we need.*

A couple of weeks ago, we went to visit the Herbert Hoover Presidential Library. On the complex, they have the home that he grew up in; it was a one-bedroom, one-living room/dining room "house," with a kitchen out back. Five people lived in Herbert Hoover's home. The entire home would literally fit inside the living room of the two-thousand-plus-square-foot house from which I'm writing this book. Three of us live in our home, and there are times it feels like we "need" more space. We might want more space, but we sure as heck don't need more space.

Have some sympathy for yourself and your partner. It is hard to sort out our needs from our wants, because we have an entire industry dedicated to manipulating us to think that our wants *are* our needs. We are saturated with messages on a moment-by-moment basis with highly effective, psychologically based propaganda influencing us to believe that we need extraneous and unnecessary stuff. It's no wonder we all get confused.

## Dealing with Disagreements

Everybody fights. We all run up against having to share limited resources. If you have married the love of your lifetime, chances are you have significant personality differences. There's a reason why opposites attract. Maybe it's because we're trying to resolve unresolved issues with our primary relationships growing up. Maybe it's simply because subconsciously we are really smart. We know we have strengths and weaknesses, and we look for somebody whose strengths complement our weaknesses. While both Winter and I have creative personalities, she is a detailed, analytical person. I am a big-picture, visionary guy whose desk could be a fascinating PhD project for an anthropological archaeological dig. The chaos I am capable and happy to function in drives Winter crazy. When you are this different, it's impossible not to rub against each other in ways that create negative friction as well as positive.

The question is not whether or not we have disagreements but how we deal with them when they come up. Is it a power struggle in which neither of us is willing to cede ground? Are we always right and he or she always wrong? Or are we in this together, equal partners in a team always looking for the ways in which both of us get what we most need? I stand by what I said at the start of this book: "Winter and I don't fight." We are a team that works together to get through whatever obstacles and challenges life throws at us, always seeking the best for each other as individuals and as a unit.

## Listen, Identify and Meet Needs

How do we do it? We listen, identify needs, and work together to meet each other's needs. It isn't always clean. It's not always pretty. We both have feelings, and when one or the other's or both of our feelings are hurt, sometimes there's a need for some time out before reengaging. But we care deeply for each other. Neither has any desire for the other to be hurt or unhappy. We trust each other to have both of our best interests at heart at all times. With the goal of mutual contentment and joy in mind, we have always been able to get there.

## Listening

Note that our process begins with listening. We both have strong personalities and are pretty bright people. We have strong opinions and have arrived at most of them for good reasons. Thus, we both have a tendency to believe we are right. "Why would you think any differently than me?" is our default thinking. Given this, it takes a conscious, deliberate effort (at least for me) to close the mouth, engage the ears, and really listen. Listening does not mean looking for points of weakness in the argument so I can get in my zingers to win. Listening does not mean waiting for her to stop talking so I can start. Nor does it mean half-listening while running through all of the thoughts and arguments in my mind that I will present as soon as she's finished. Listening means putting aside my agenda and really trying to figure out where Winter is coming from. More often than not, it means asking questions like, "This is what I think I'm hearing. Am I understanding correctly?" or "Tell me more about what this means."

Here's the really cool thing. When we focus on listening and understand where our partner is coming from, we tend to forget all our arguments for being right, and our deepest needs percolate to the surface. So, not only does our partner get what he or she needs most, which is that you really hear where he or she is coming from, but listening is this wonderful sifting process separating

> *When we focus on listening and understand where our partner is coming from, we tend to forget all our arguments for being right, and our deepest needs percolate to the surface.*

the wheat from the chaff. All our arguments about how I am right and you are wrong tend to get left in the bowl while our deepest needs are sitting there, looking at you in the sieve.

There's more. Listening and focusing on where our partner is coming from tends to reduce our anxiety. It's hard to be wrapped up in what I'm thinking or feeling when my focus is on trying to understand where Winter is coming from.

## Together and Apart

One of the great challenges of being in a relationship together is how to be separate and apart; true, strong, independent individuals who are also together. How do we work to be interdependent, not codependent and enmeshed, nor disengaged and unconnected? How do we connect together deeply as a couple and have space and room to fully develop as individuals? It's no wonder when our partner is thinking something vastly different from us that we feel anxious. It matters. It matters a lot. What does this mean for you? What does this mean for me? What does this mean for us? The tendency we all have is to try to get our partner to think like us. "If you don't agree with me, how do we move forward?" If your partner always has to think like you, then who are they as an individual? If you always have to agree with your partner in order to stay together, who are you?

Winter and I just watched *The Runaway Bride*. This is a really interesting romantic comedy illustrating precisely this challenge. Julia Roberts's character can never "seal the deal." She has abandoned four suitors literally at the altar. What is slowly revealed in the movie is that she doesn't know who she is. In each relationship, she takes on the favorite activities, food, hobbies, etc. of her partner. The primary metaphor for this in the movie is eggs: with one fiancé, her favorite is poached; with another, it's egg whites; with another, it's scrambled with herbs. When she finally takes time and figures out who she is, independent of a partner, then she can commit and follow through on her marriage to Richard Gere's character.

Independent, fully realized as individuals, each with his or her own interests, hobbies, and passions, *and* together, deeply committed to a partnership with shared interests, hobbies, and passions. It's a tricky, tricky balance. When a disagreement comes up, of course we feel anxious! We're together. What happens if we're different? Well, of course we're different. That's a large part of what we like about each other. Different parts that fit together physically, emotionally, and spiritually sometimes leads to ecstatic union, other times to caustic differences.

One of the keys to working through the sometimes painfully challenging differences is listening. One way to help ourselves listen is thinking about this as a quest. We are looking to identify the source of pain our partner is experiencing. What we are hearing on the surface is more often than not a symptom of a more deep-seated, hidden pain. In the aforementioned example of the toilet seat, I never heard my ex-wife's pain. To this day, I have no clue what that was all about for her. Was it "splashing down" for her or something else? Maybe, having grown up with all sisters, she'd never had to deal with a toilet seat in any other position than down. I will never know because I never asked. I never listened to her about the toilet seat.

## Exercise 5: Listening Exercise

Identify a silly issue that you argue about regularly with your partner. If you don't have a partner, practice with a father, mother, sister, or brother. Choose something like the toilet seat or which way the toilet paper is supposed to come off the roll, an issue that in the grand scheme of things is small potatoes. Practice listening. You can begin the conversation with something like, "We've always argued about this thing. Could you tell me what that's all about for you?" Listen. Remember that you have a quest. An investigation to accomplish that cannot be wrapped up until you have identified his or her pain. You will have to ask questions. You will have to probe deeper. There's probably more going on than what is on the surface. What are your clues?

What seems to be eliciting an emotional response from your partner? Did they just say, "You always …"? If you are like me, you are tempted to jump in and make a correction: "That's not right. I don't always leave the toilet seat up. I remembered just yesterday. I left it down for a whole two hours! Ha! See? I'm right. You're wrong." Stop! It is almost never the case that any of us "always" does anything. When someone else is saying, "You always ..." this is an expression of frustration and a clue. Aha, you're getting somewhere. What's that about? Say something like, "I hear that you are feeling really frustrated or angry about *xyz*. Am I right? Tell me more. I really want to understand." Listen some more.

**Ask for clarification**. Are there points you really don't understand? "I understand you feel it's wrong to leave the toilet seat up, but I don't understand how this affects you. What about this feels wrong to you?"

**Mirror and match.** After your partner has expressed how he or she is feeling, repeat back to your partner what was just said to you in your own words. If your partner says, "It's wrong to leave the toilet seat up," say something like, "I understand you feel it's wrong for me to leave the toilet seat up." This does a number of things. One, it shows your partner you are really listening. Two, it gives them an opportunity to make corrections and clarifications or to go deeper like, "It's wrong because it gets piss everywhere, and it's disgusting, and I'm stuck cleaning up after you."

Aha! There's more here than meets the eye, isn't there? There are a couple of issues going on. There's the aesthetic one of how dried urine on a toilet seat looks and smells and the issue of feeling stuck doing work that I'm not responsible for.

**Name the issues.** "I think I'm hearing a couple of things going on here. There's the appearance and smell of the toilet, and it sounds like you're feeling like I'm not doing my share of some of the work around the house. Is that right?" When you start getting toward the real pain, your partner will let you know. It will sound something like, "Yes! I always feel like I have to do everything around the house!" Your investigation is now bearing real fruit. Look at all that exaggeration. That, my friend, is real frustration and pain. Stay in the pocket. When you hit the pay dirt of a gusher of real pain, you are going to want to stop the flow of it because you are going to feel it too, and we all want to avoid pain. Don't.

**Tell your partner what you've just heard.** "I'm hearing you feel really mad, that you don't feel like I'm stepping up to the plate with work around the house, and you feel responsible for seeing that it all gets done. Is that right? Is there more?"

**Apologize.** At any point, and especially when you find the pain, you can always sincerely apologize. Apologizing is not necessarily an admission of guilt or that are you wrong. It is acknowledging that something that you did created pain for your partner. You are not responsible for that feeling; they are. We are all responsible for our own feelings, but saying, "Wow. I see that *xyz* really hurt you. I'm sorry. I don't want you to feel hurt," acknowledges how they are feeling and a wish for something different.

Your objective when you have discovered the root of the pain is to listen to the effect this pain has on your partner and to help them tell you about that until they can't think of anything more. It is at this point that your partner has revealed their deepest need, and you have helped them discover it. You have cared for them simply by listening. That is a job well done. Good work!

Some "go to" questions or statements for listening:

"Tell me more."

"Tell me about that.

"Could you tell me about ...?"

"What concerns you about ...?"

"What is most important about this to you?"

"What else?"

"Is there more?"

## Challenging Work

When someone you care for comes at you with real anger and pain and they direct that anger at you, it will engage your "lizard brain"—the part of all of us that is reactive, defensive and instinctual. You are going to want to do one of two things—fight or flee. It's going to happen. You won't even think about it until after the fact. This is where the phrase, "Open mouth, insert foot" comes from. You'll be cruising along in your conversation, listening well. As soon as that raw, undoctored, unfiltered pain from your partner hits you, "Wham!"—it feels like a shot in the gut. All the wind goes out of you, and suddenly you either find yourself retreating and hiding in your turtle shell or coming back with your own zinger. Oops.

Stop. Breathe. I mean literally. Take a deep breath. Take another. You need to get yourself out of the instinctual part of your brain and back into the thinking side. Count backward from ten. Remember—this is what you were looking for: pain. This is a clue. To get to win-win, you have to get at the root of the issue. If you have already reacted, immediately apologize and reaffirm what you are working toward. Say something like, "I'm sorry. I really do want to hear where you are coming from." Then go back to asking an open-ended question.

## Time Out

If your partner has really managed to hit you in a tender spot, you might need to call for a time out. A good shot to the emotional gut can render you incapable of getting back into your thinking brain. The lizard brain has taken over, and you have become Godzilla. Before you go stomping around, tearing up the town, stepping on cars and knocking down buildings, call for a time out by saying, "I need a break." Set a time limit: "Can we come back in half an hour?" Go for a walk. Go for a run. Go to the fitness club and beat on the heavy bag. Listen to music. Do whatever you need to do away from your partner, and be Godzilla alone until you reach the point that you are able to actually think again and start asking yourself open-ended questions: "What am I so mad about? Why am I hurt? What am I afraid of? What's the need I have?" All these will help you return to the mild-mannered Bruce Banner scientist/investigator that you are (Okay, I know I'm mixing my metaphors, but

> *A good shot to the emotional gut can render you incapable of getting back into your thinking brain. The lizard brain has taken over, and you have become Godzilla.*

the Hulk and Godzilla are both big, green, destructive, and completely irrational. Coincidence? I think not.)

## Your Turn

After your partner has shared with you all they've got, and you've repeated back in your own words what they have said, and both of you know that you really understand where the other is coming from, then it is your turn. To continue with our toilet seat example, you have found that two things are at issue for your partner: they feel that a urine-covered toilet is disgusting, and they are frustrated with the distribution of labor around the house. How do you think and feel? Maybe you grew up in a urine-covered bathroom, and that feels like home to you. Weird. Gross, maybe, but it's you. If you are like me, now that you have actively listened to your partner, mined for pain, and sought deeply to understand, most if not all your arguments about who is right and who is wrong have gone out the window, and you are left with your deepest need: "I need to feel like my house is my home." Now you can share with your partner what is your deepest need, and you can begin the work of figuring out how to work toward win-win.

## Coming Together

How do you work toward win-win, where you both get what you need—not what you want, but what you need? There is some give and take here. You might recognize that, in this case, a urine-covered bathroom may not be the best way to achieve a feeling of home if you ever want to live with somebody else—ever. There are other ways to make a house feel like a home. Your partner wants the house to feel like home too. Aha, a point of agreement! In fact, when you both think about it, the issue you were both discussing really was, "How do we make our house feel like a home? How do we share the work of home-making? What does home look, act, and feel like, for us together and as individuals?" When you get to this stage, it's time for brainstorming.

## Exercise 6: Brainstorming Exercise

- Try to list at least ten possible solutions to the problem. During brainstorming, it is important not to judge or criticize any ideas. In fact, it is sometimes helpful to begin with some that are completely outlandish. Think outside the box, because it primes the creative pump. While the outlandish ideas may not be viable as a solution, there are often elements in them that can be included in the best solution you want to try. You wouldn't have thought of them if you hadn't begun on the fringes of possibility.
- Discuss and evaluate each possible solution. Be as objective as possible. Talk about how useful and appropriate each suggestion feels for resolving your issue.
- Agree on one solution to try.
- Agree how you will each work toward this solution. Be as specific as possible. What will you do? What will he or she do?
- Set up another meeting to discuss your progress.
- Give positive feedback to each other for progress. If you notice your partner making a positive

contribution toward the solution, praise his or her effort. You might even thank your partner![7]

## Trust

Trust is the foundation on which everything else in a relationship is built—everything. We cannot communicate well without trust. We cannot share well without trust. We cannot live well together without trust. Without trust, our relationship is a broken vessel. It is a sieve that cannot hold the emotional lifeblood of our relationship. Trust is the benchmark of a relationship. Do everything, and I mean everything, you possibly can to establish, nurture, grow, and sustain trust—all the time, every time. Trust is unbelievably fragile. It is easily broken and once broken, really, really, *really* hard to get back again—ever.

This is not to say that we won't or don't hurt each other. With different personalities; different families of origin; different expectations for life; and different wants, needs, and desires, it is virtually impossible to not hurt each other from time to time. Do I trust that my partner does not want to hurt me, has my best interests at heart, and truly, deeply cares for me? This is the essence of trust and love, and it is something that has to be experienced in order to be felt.

## The Emotional Bank

Remember—love is an action, not a feeling. Nobody knows how we feel. The way people in our lives know how we feel is through our behavior. This has been pointed out to me by my lovely wife in a number of particular ways. I am crazy

---

[7] Paraphrased from Prepare/Enrich, "Couple's Workbook" www. prepare-enrich.com © Copyright 2008 Life Innovations, Inc., 9.

in love with Winter and my kids. There is nothing more important to me than them. This is how I feel. There are ways I succeed in expressing these feelings, and there are ways I fail. Here are some examples.

**Success**: Every day is Valentine's Day. I profess this and try to live it every day. Every day is a good day to give Winter flowers. Every day is a good day to make breakfast in bed. Every day is a day to wake up and say to Winter and Ella (my youngest daughter, still living with us), "Good morning, beautiful! I am so grateful to have you in my life. Thank you!"

**Failure**: I have evening meetings all the time. Not a week goes by that I don't have at least one meeting on one night of the week. For too many years, I have given Winter an ETA as to what time the meeting will be over, and then the meeting runs over, and I fail to let her know that I'm running late. This is not caring for her. I have made her a kind of promise—when I will be home—and then not followed through.

I did not really understand that this was not loving until one day Winter said to me, "I know that you love me, but it does not feel like that to me. When you tell me that you are going to be home and then you aren't home at that time, it does not matter how you feel. You may feel sorry. You may feel regret. You may feel like you

> *"I don't know what you feel.
> I only know what you do."*

love me, but you are not treating me with love. I don't know what you feel. I only know what you do."

Now, I had read and listened to Stephen Covey's *7 Habits of Highly Effective People* multiple times at that point. I had heard him say over and over again, "Love is an action." I had preached numerous sermons saying exactly the same thing. I had lived "every day is Valentine's Day" for years, but I really didn't get "love is an action" until that concrete failure was staring me in the face. It really is the little things.

This was not a big deal. I was not having an affair or drinking until three in the morning and calling for Winter to bring me home every night. It was a question of, "Do you follow through on what you say you are going to do or not? Do you love me like that?" It is a big deal. Love is an action.

In *7 Habits of Highly Effective People*, Covey talks about the "emotional bank account" that lives in all of us. We all receive and give "deposits" and "withdrawals." A deposit in the account might look like making a commitment or promise and following through, being kind, or apologizing. A withdrawal might be a put-down, not following through, or criticizing or complaining about someone when they are not there. Deposits result in growing trust. When we make regular deposits into the emotional bank account, trust grows, communication becomes easy, and we feel like we have a safe, solid, strong relationship. Regular withdrawals with no deposits result in steadily increasing suspicion, hurt and anger, and less communication. When communication happens, it is more and more "political"—i.e., suspicious and guarded.

What you and your partner do is what creates your feelings. Far and away the most popular Bible story for a wedding comes from 1 Corinthians 13. It goes, "Love is patient; love is kind; love is not envious or boastful or arrogant or rude. It does not insist on its own way; it is not irritable or resentful; it does not rejoice in wrongdoing, but rejoices in the truth. It bears all things, believes all things, hopes all things, endures all things. Love never ends." Notice that Paul's description of love does not refer to a single feeling. Each descriptor is an action and describes a "deposit" in the emotional bank. The action precedes and creates the feeling. Feelings are dependent on behavior. Do these things, and you and your partner will feel love.

If you want to feel more love, act more loving. If your relationship is feeling dry and passionless, do something that is passionate and do it more frequently. If you want to feel more trust, be more trustworthy.

Trust and communication are the anchors of keeping the love of a lifetime. They depend on each other. More trust equals more open, easy communication. Less trust equals less open and easy communication. If we marry our best friend, these two elements are easy, but they can also be easily blown. We can take a great relationship with our best friend, but if we don't make regular deposits in the emotional bank account, if we don't treat our partner with love and care on a regular basis, if we are not trustworthy, the person who was once our best friend will become something else.

## Fight Fairly

In one of my churches, a member came up to Winter and said, "I don't know what's wrong with my husband. He's always raising his voice when he's angry and I told him it's wrong to do that."

Winter said, "Well, everybody raises their voice sometimes."

She said, "No! No, it's wrong! You and Tom don't raise your voices ever."

Winter responded, "Sometimes we do."

"No! No, you don't!" she said, getting more and more upset the longer the conversation continued.

Winter said, "Umm ... I better go check on Ella."

As I said earlier, there is friction in every relationship. The question is not whether or when there will be disagreements; the question is how we deal with disagreements and the challenges that present themselves. The truth is, a truly good fight where we work together to find a mutually agreeable solution that feels like a win-win strengthens the relationship, as opposed to weakening it. When you fight, fight fairly. Here are some dos and don'ts.

## <u>Do</u>

- Care for your partner, no matter how you are feeling.
- Talk about how you feel.
- Use "I" phrases, not "you" phrases. For example: I wish, I want, I feel, I hope.
- Open your ears, close your mouth.
- Use active listening.
- If at any point, you feel strongly that you are about to do one of the "don'ts" listed below, ask for a time out.
- When asking for a time out, always include an approximate time when you will return to the discussion.

**Don't**

- Cuss, curse, or use abusive language.
- Throw things.
- Threaten.
- Hit, slap, or be physically abusive in any way.
- Yell or scream.
- Use absolutes like "always" or "never."

If you consistently follow through with the above, chances are good that you will be able to honestly say, as I do, "My spouse and I never fight. We disagree, sometimes passionately, but we don't fight."

Here are two exercises paraphrased directly from Prepare-Enrich (www.prepare-enrich.com, *Couple's Workbook* 2008, 4, 9) on how to fight fair and work toward win-win.

## Exercise 7: Creating a Wish List

Create a wish list of things that you want more or less of in your relationship. This is a variation on an evaluation exercise I do with every project I work on: 1) What's good/what do we want to do more of? 2) What's bad/what do we wish never happened again? 3) What needs to be tweaked/what can be improved?

This exercise will also give you an opportunity to work on your communication skills. Remember to use the skills you learned in the listening exercise and to be assertive in asking for what you want in your relationship and clearly expressing how you feel.

Work separately and create your lists alone. After you each have created your lists, get together and take turns sharing your lists with each other.

*First: Write down three things that you would either like to do more of, never do again, or want to improve in your relationship.

1) _____

_____

2) _____

_____

3) _____

_____

*Second: Sit down together. Decide who will go first. He or she will then share the first item on his or her list. Alternate back and forth, each sharing one item on your list until each of you has worked through your list.

- When sharing your wish, remember to use "I" statements: I wish … I want … I feel …" and share how you would feel if your wish came true.
- When listening to your partner's wish, remember to say back what the wish is and how your partner would feel if their wish came true in your own words.

## Exercise 8: Conflict Resolution

Every couple has differences and disagreements. As I said earlier, a well-resolved disagreement where everybody feels listened to and had their deepest needs honored and respected strengthens the relationship. This exercise can be used repeatedly, helping to resolve conflict and avoid common, destructive behaviors.

1. Choose a time and place to discuss the issue.

2. Clearly define the challenge. Be specific. _____

_____

3. List the ways you each contribute to the challenge.

Partner 1: _____

_____

Partner 2: _____

_____

4. List all the ways you have tried to resolve the issue before:

    1)

    2)

    3)

    4)

5. Use the brainstorming process on pg. 82

Winter: This chapter is really quite simple. Follow through on the small things, and your partner will trust you to follow through on the large things. I like to give Thomas the things he needs and desires. It makes my heart happy. I know he feels the same toward me. If you do your best to give your partner what they need, and if they are a caring individual, they will feel loved and honored and will want to give you what you most want and need.

# Chapter 7

# Take It to the Show

So, you've found the love of your lifetime. You've successfully wooed him or her. You are married. You're doing all
the right stuff. You fight well. You enjoy each other's company. It's fourteen years later. Do you still feel the same way?
Deeper? More? Or are you feeling bored? The "seven-year
itch" getting to you? How do you keep the fire burning?

Countless people look at how Winter and I act together
and say things like, "Are you two newlyweds?" We have been
married sixteen years, and I can honestly say virtually every
day, I love Winter more—and this appears to be mutual.
Perhaps more than anything else, this seems to elicit the
question, "How do you do it?" Here's how.

## Take Every Opportunity to Enjoy Loving Your Partner

Do you remember how you felt the first time you saw your
partner, talked to him or her, and thought, *Ooh, there's something here I want to check out*? Do you remember your first

date? Those first months of falling in love? It felt pretty
good, didn't it? If you are a guy, you brought flowers, not
because you were in trouble but because you just wanted to
offer a small gift to make her happy. You opened doors.
Maybe you wrote poetry or brought chocolates. You were on
your best behavior at all times. Everything was new. It was all
a rush! The world was brighter. Your senses were heightened.
New love is the best drug of all. Does that have to end?

I say, "No!" I hear countless people putting down their
partners or allowing daily living to take the spice and joy
and breathtaking moments out of their relationships. *Don't
do it!*

Life is too short. When I was in my midtwenties, I noticed
that life seemed to be speeding up. The days, months, and
years seemed to be going by faster and faster. I was in my
first job as a pastor. I was surrounded by older people, so
I began sharing this observation with my elders and asked
them, "Does it ever slow down?" The answer was, "No. It
just keeps going faster and faster." Life is too short to waste
a second not appreciating the love of a lifetime.

## The Secret

This is the love of your life. Take every opportunity to actively love him or her. If there is one secret to falling in love
more and more every day, to looking like you are newlyweds fifty years later, I think this is it. This is what Winter
and I do. We take as many opportunities as we can to show
that we love each other. We play and laugh and tease each
other constantly. We appreciate the way each other looks
and moves and feels. We hold hands and are always touching
each other. I bring Winter flowers often, not because I'm in

trouble, but because she's had a bad day or a good day, or just because I know she likes flowers.

We try to be gentle with each other's sore spots. Winter can't stand clutter or mess, so I try to keep my clothes picked up from the side of the bed and do not allow the dishes to pile up in the sink. (Anybody who has lived with me knows what a seismic shift in behavior this is!) She makes dinner often when I have a late night at work.

We try to allow each other to work from our strengths and not allow society's or anybody else's expectations get in the way. When Ella was three or four, she was telling her grandfather the story of the Three Bears. The ending always made Ella sad, so she embellished the end of the story with, "And the momma bear fixed all the furniture and the poppa bear made some more porridge."

Her grandfather said, "Don't you mean the poppa bear fixed the furniture and the momma bear made the porridge?"

Ella replied, "Silly Grandpa. That doesn't how it goes!"

We consistently ensure that there is at least one day we take off of work every week, and often use at least some of that time to go on a date together. These might include reading to each other or playing games or checking out a distillery on the river or a museum or a library—whatever sounds like fun together.

We don't only set aside special date time. From throwing socks at each other when folding laundry (socking each other) to board games to remembering every e-mail is an opportunity to

*play together every day in every way*

send a playful love note like "Hello, my sweet love muffin of passion," we play together every day in every way. (I can almost hear readers everywhere thinking, "Uck! Gag me with a spoon!" You're right. The e-mail is ridiculous, over the top, tongue planted firmly in cheek. That's the point. I know Winter laughs, often out loud when she receives an e-mail addressing her like this. I certainly do when I receive one from her.) The point is we play together—a lot!

We give each other space and time to pursue our individual hobbies and passions. I practice the martial art Aikido and spend most Monday evenings engaged in that activity. I support Winter in her hobby, which has become a home-based business. She sculpts doll food out of polymer clay and sells it online through an Etsy shop and her website. (If you or your kids or grandchildren have American Girl or Barbie or any other doll and would like some food for them to play with, check out FauxRealFood.com. She is an amazingly talented artist. In fact, people often cannot discern pictures of her food sculptures from pictures of real food!) We shamelessly promote each other.

We never put each other down, not in private or in public. We don't participate in the apparently socially acceptable game of dissing your partner or members of the opposite sex. Whenever I hear "the boys" talking about how women are always talking too long, I say, "Well, more often than not, Winter and Ella are stuck waiting for me because I'm in the middle of talking to you!" We make it easy for each other to not participate in those games because, more often than not, those stereotypes are not accurate to our relationship.

**Winter's Two Cents**: Worst advice? Forget about it. In our culture, if someone does us a favor, we often respond with, "Forget about it." Forget about it! Really? It's a terrible saying! Why would you want to forget about the ways people treat you well? Instead, do your best to remember all the kindnesses paid by your partner (and everyone else too). Instead, try to forget about the minor inconveniences and infractions. I'm not suggesting you ignore them or deny real pain, but after you've adequately dealt with it, try to let it go. I promise you'll feel more warmly toward your partner, and you'll both be happier.

An example: I'm visually oriented, and clutter bugs me. Thomas occasionally forgets his dirty clothes on the floor at his bedside. Do I berate him for it, saying, "You never listen to me. You just do that to bug me"? Absolutely not! I choose to remember all the nights he has surprised me by quietly folding the laundry. He forgot his socks on the floor; so what? Big deal. More often than not, this man comes home after work and folds all the laundry.

He's aware that clothes on the floor bother me, and I know he tries to remember to put them in the hamper. I quietly pick up his things and put them away. On the days when I do feel annoyed, I make a mental list of all the sweet things Thomas does for me. That exercise always leaves me feeling grateful.

Remember the nice things. Do your best to let go of the annoyances and problems after you've dealt with them.

One last word of advice: if you don't like the way your relationship is going, if there are some things that you would like to change, change your behavior. Don't read a bunch of self-help books like this one and try to use them to get your partner to change. I remember

> *if you don't like the way your relationship is going, if there are some things that you would like to change, change your behavior*

reading, *Men Are from Mars, Women Are from Venus* together with my ex-wife. We were trying to figure out how to improve our struggling relationship. It's a good book, which we then used as a club on each other, trying to get the other to change. Don't do this!

There's a reason the genre is titled "self-help." It's to work on changing ourselves, not someone else. Use self-help books to figure out the things you would like to change about *you*. The cool thing is, if we change, over time our relationship and our partner will change. It really is just like dancing together. If we consistently, regularly over time change the dance we are doing, our partner will eventually change their steps. At first, it's going to be ugly. You'll be stepping all over each other. Your partner will wonder what the heck you're doing and in all probability will try to get you to go back to the dance you are both most familiar with. But if you're tired of the waltz you're doing together, try salsa or merengue. Eventually, they'll come along, especially if it's a dance that's more fun and healthy.

## The Last Exercises

- Make a list of things you love about your partner.
  - o Make a schedule for yourself of when you tell him or her each thing; at least one every day. Could be first thing in the morning, last thing at night, a phone call in the middle of the day.
- Identify a date night with your partner.
  - o At least once per month, so that you can consistently follow through.
  - o Brainstorm together what you would like to do on your dates.
- Figure out one small thing your partner loves receiving—flowers, chocolates, cards, hugs, kisses, etc. Give it to him or her as often as is reasonably possible.
- Kiss your partner when you leave and when your partner comes home. Stop what you are doing, smile at them. Give them a warm kiss and a hug.

My deepest wish and blessing for you is that you find, keep, and revel in the love of your lifetime.

# Gratitude

## (AKA Acknowledgements)

I cannot express the depth of my gratitude for my lovely wife Winter; my primary partner, consultant, advisor, supporter, encourager, and accountability partner for this book and the rest of life. You make life sweet!

A big thank you to Bill Selby with the Center for Pastoral Effectiveness. What an amazing mentor you are in being a 'non-anxious presence', active listening and self-care. Echoes of you resound throughout the book especially in "Exercise 4: Personal and Family Stuff."

Thanks to Tim Zimmer. You have been an awesome sounding board for all things regarding business development. Thank you for all the ways that you help me grow. You are a wonderful friend.

Thanks to Mom and Dad for your love, care and support through the years.

Big thank you to my kids, Mario, Nina and Ella and grandsons Thomas and Gio. You are all things bright and beautiful! True gifts from God!

For all my friends, and partners in life, the church and business that I have not specifically named. In significant ways, you wrote this with me. I carry you with me at all times as you have shaped and formed who I am.

Peace,

Tom

# About the Author

Tom Boomershine is the founder of EcoSphere Coaching, a life and executive coaching business focusing on overcoming challenges in communication. Soon to be certified in Judith E. Glaser's Conversational Intelligence and as an Associate Certified Coach by the International Coaching Federation, Tom coaches both individuals and organizations to bridge communication challenges created by differences in culture and personalities.

To my readers, I have a special offer. My greatest hope is that you are able to find and keep the love of your life. So, readers of "After Ever After" are entitled to one hour of life coaching *at no cost*. I will coach you on any of the exercises or issues from the book on which you would like to work. Because you are my treasured reader, we can also work on any other life or work issue you desire to address. Just email me at tboomershine@mac.com and put "After Ever After reader" in the subject line.